T0243461

Peak Season

Peak
Season

12 Months of Recipes Celebrating
Ontario's Freshest Ingredients

Deirdre Buryk

Foreword by Ran Goel

appetite

Appetite by Random House® and colophon are registered trademarks
of Penguin Random House LLC.

Library and Archives Canada Cataloguing in Publication is available upon request.
ISBN: 9780525611691
eBook ISBN: 9780525611707

Cover and interior design: Leah Springate
Interior photography: Janette Downie
Interior photography on pages vi, ix, 3, 4, 18, 22, 24, 32, 45, 47, 63, 68, 71, 103, 104, 128, 137, 150, 153,
155, 167, 169, 170, 189, 193, 194, 201, 221, 224, 231, 237, 247, 252, 254, 276 by Deirdre Buryk
Cover and interior photography styling: Deirdre Buryk
Interior illustrations: Candice Silver

Printed in China

Published in Canada by Appetite by Random House®,
a division of Penguin Random House Canada Limited.

www.penguinrandomhouse.ca

10 9 8 7 6 5 4 3 2 1

For Dad (1950–2010) and Mom.

And a note of thanks

*I have learned from many people with great wisdom of
the region—farmers, foragers, food producers, chefs, and food experts
(historians), though I'd be remiss not to say it is Indigenous Peoples
who are the real stewards of Ontario. This land is currently home to
Indigenous Peoples from across Turtle Island, is traditional territory of the
Haudenosaunee, the Anishinaabe, and the Wendat, and is the territory
of the Mississaugas of the Credit. Indigenous Peoples hold every gift
of the land as sacred. Without plants, animals, and resources,
humanity would not exist.*

Contents

Spring

Summer

Fall

Winter

Foreword

WHAT DO YOU NEED TO KNOW about the author of this beautiful book, Deirdre Buryk? I met her in the expiring days of the fifth growing season of our urban farm in Toronto. In the years since, she has become one of Fresh City's chief culinary architects, helping us with our locally and organically sourced prepared food and meal kit programs. She is one of the most unique people I have encountered. There is a serene joy in how Dee, as I know her, approaches the world. This is not that synthetic, exaggerated optimism you may have come across in some. Hers is authentic and unassuming. Her default sensibility is one of joy, of wonder, and of the possible. That makes her the perfect tour guide to the Ontario growing season. She comes at the act of eating from a place of abundance. Eating with the seasons is not about sacrifice or limitations. It is about exploring what our own backyards have in store for us. And it is fundamentally about the rhythms of nature, at once alien and yet still primally familiar, even to us moderns. Each of us, if we stop and listen, will hear something different. For me, the early days of the season are the best time, with the promise of long, sunny days ahead, and thoughts of crisp, overwintered spinach just a few weeks away. For you, it may be the many rewards of August, when the plethora of crops seeded back in the spring finally reach maturity. And for all of us, eating with the seasons instills a sense of gratitude for what is before us and a humility about a cycle that preceded and will outlive us. Dee teases out the beauty of the bounty that the soil of Ontario blesses us with. And she concocts recipes that are as unpretentious and accessible as they are delicious. I suspect you will find between these covers inspiration and joy for many growing seasons to come.

Ran Goel
Founder & CEO, Fresh City Farms

Introduction

Peak Season IS A STORY ABOUT what I've learned as my relationship to this land has deepened. Through my years of cooking, I have learned a lot about the food that grows in Ontario. Paying closer attention, I now realize how vibrant these fruits and vegetables are. This is a book—in fact, a love letter—about these gifts and the home that has provided it to me. Ontario is a province with wildly diverse flavours and people, with an ever-changing balance of seasons—a place that I believe should be a culinary destination. Sure, we are young when it comes to documenting our food history—maybe even a toddler stumbling in a world of grown-up regions like Oaxaca, Hong Kong, or Bologna—but Ontario is particularly special. From my experience visiting farms, we have twelve distinct growing seasons—each with its own identity. Categorizing our climate into spring, summer, fall, and winter doesn't seem to fit the bill when each month bears new ingredients at their freshest in, well, *peak season*. It's like having your very own culinary muse in your backyard (or balcony garden in my case). Take a tomato, for example—so simple—plucked off the vine and eaten with just a sprinkle of sea salt. Or perhaps, drizzled with an herb oil and placed on a hunk of warm baguette in August—not November, not April—under the hot summer sun. By the time an ingredient goes out of season, something else, like a rich, nutty sunchoke—ready to relax into a velvety autumn soup—is in season, and the spirit of that August tomato will be a pleasant memory for next year.

Instead of tethering myself to a particular recipe and hunting down each specific ingredient, I prefer to cook by the season. It is a magic trick, really. Whatever may be in peak season is also going to be full of flavour and that vegetable fortitude is hard to mess up. Though, there is creativity needed for this. This type of cooking requires adapting to what is available and will always buoy a playful side to my cooking. I didn't always cook with such intimacy. I spent much of my career teaching, counselling, and learning how to eat "optimally," using the precision of numbers as a nutritionist. When I started developing recipes in my test kitchen, years ago, at Fresh City Farms and in my more recent years coordinating the Leslieville Farmers' Market, I began to broaden my relationships with food grown in Ontario and with those who grow it. The farmers I know have always been my greatest culinary teachers. I began to understand food a little more with every farmer I visited. A rooted carrot would be plucked out of the soil and urged to try. They would show me how a radish isn't *just* a radish, but comes in many forms and spectrums of spice. How a new spring turnip is delicate and sweet, flavours best preserved by steaming instead of roasting. You may think you know what spinach tastes like, but nothing can be as healing as this verdant green picked straight from the field. If I could give you that perfect bunch of spinach that looks and feels alive, you would experience the meaning and wholesomeness of peak flavour—not even the most exotic superfood can compete with that. This is the foundation of cooking simply, connecting to home, eating with intent, and developing a deeper appreciation of how food gets to your plate. When I stopped trying to control the ingredients I wanted to use and let the repeating cycles of monthly vegetables and fruits inspire me, the more intuitive I became in the kitchen, and I hope the same happens for you.

In these pages you will find a collection of my favourite recipes made mostly from plants and inspired by this province's flourishing seasons. Every season—and every month—presents a diverse ensemble of fruits and vegetables, each with their own charming personalities. I like to keep my cooking simple and casual. When I cook at home, I cook in a relaxed, sensorial way that would probably raise eyebrows in my test kitchen. These recipes are more influenced by my home cooking than they are by my recipe development career. They are not definitive, and I invite you to use each one as a starting point to a new way of eating.

Whether you are looking for a quick, delicious meal or a sensational affair on a plate, there is something for everyone here and for all types of occasions. Most are easy recipes for those whose time is short, though I did sprinkle in some more involved recipes—such as mushroom-garlic pot-stickers for family night, a slow-cooked brisket during the high holidays, or a multi-layered carrot cake filled with Ontario walnuts and ground cherries to celebrate a special someone's birthday. These recipes take a little extra time because the ritual of making them deserves as much attention as the ingredients themselves. These types of traditions create magical moments that I, like many, carry forever.

Some recipes I hold near and dear to my heart are from my grandma, my aunts, my mother, and my father, while many are inspired by friends, teachers, and loved ones who have welcomed me into their kitchens and showed me the heart of their cuisine—and lucky for me, in Toronto, there are many cuisines to taste. As you flip through each month's recipes, it will become more and more evident that I grew up on the flavours of my hometown, Toronto, one of the most multicultural cities in the world. Dishes here are influenced by Chinese, Italian, French, Jamaican, Japanese, and Mexican cuisines, to name a few. All of these have played a major part in developing my taste buds. Just like the soil that fosters an astonishing range of fruits and vegetables, Ontario food is also inherently about celebrating an exchange of cultural diversity.

I hope this book offers you many new cooking experiences and inspires you to eat all the wonderful plants that Ontario has to offer. And more than anything, my dream is to give you an opportunity to develop a new relationship to this land, these plants, these animals, and most importantly, to one another. It doesn't matter where we are from; we all find ourselves making food as a way to live a life deliberately full of love and kindness.

A Monthly Guide to Ontario's Peak Produce

IF SOMEONE WERE TO TELL ME that I could freely walk into a food emporium brimming with any vegetable or fruit my heart desires, at any given time—say, blueberries or summer squash, even in February—I would call that paradise. Or so I believed until I remembered what that blueberry tastes like freshly picked in July just up the road from me. The Southern Ontario climate offers diverse conditions for a plenitude of vegetables year-round. But when the only sign of a change in seasons in the produce aisle is the appearance of rare May fiddleheads, it is all too easy to forget how precious, even flavourful, a particular ingredient can be.

There are 12 months in a year, and in each of those months, Ontario bears new ingredients that reflect the season and distinctive regional landscape of this province. Allow these next few pages to escort you through the seasons and inspire what to cook next. As you flip through, you will discover what Ontario looks like from March through February in the world of edible plants. Please use the breakdown of recipes here as a guideline, not a prescription, as every year varies season to season. Some springs have earlier frosts than others, so wild leeks may appear before April—if one is so lucky. You won't find every Ontario vegetable or fruit here, but these recipes offer a good starting point and celebrate some of my favourite ingredients. I like to be specific about the freshness of ingredients used, but feel free to adjust to your own palate, dietary needs, economics, and geographical location. Please use each recipe as a guide, not a rule. There is something for every taste bud, and plenty of ways to fine tune the dishes to your needs.

Spring | March

Sugar maples are ready to tap, spring mushrooms are popping up, and the frost has melted. Sing to the high heavens and use up the last of your storage vegetables (rainbow carrots, butternut squash, red onions, and hardy greens), because spring is on its way.

Beets (no tops)

Cabbage

Carrots (no tops)

Celeriac

Chicories

Garlic

Kale

Leeks

Maple

Mushrooms

Onions

Parsnips

Potatoes

Rutabaga

Turnips

Winter Squash

Spring | April

Take a back seat, acorn squash—the first sightings of greens are peeking out of the ground. First come the two basal leaves from wild leeks. Then the striking vibrant red stalks of rhubarb appear. Next thing you know, you will be out foraging for mushrooms and fiddleheads, and markets will be adorned with new potatoes, young carrots, and spring radishes.

Angelica

Beets (with tops)

Cabbage

Carrots
(no tops)

Chicories

Fiddleheads

Garlic

Hardy Greens

Herbs (Mint)

Mushrooms

Nettles

Onions

Potatoes

Radishes

Turnips

Wild Leeks

Spring | May

Grocery lists become grander as the warmer weather arrives. Tack on asparagus, snap peas, and chives (with their blossoms) to your list. My dishes tend to be fresher and brighter—filled with the first delicate greens and covered with a whole lot of herbs like dill and mint.

Angelica

Asparagus

Chives

Dandelion

Dill

Fiddleheads

Haskap

Mushrooms (Portobello)

Mustard

Nettles

Radishes (with tops)

Rhubarb

Rutabaga

Salad Mixes

Snap Peas

Sorrel

Spinach

Watercress

Wild Leeks

Summer | June

Days are long and the fields are purple (from lavender) and green (from spiralling garlic scapes). Young vegetables, like Easter egg radishes, are timid and less pungent when picked early. Early fruits, like mulberries, line the streets; though not in stores, they are right above your hairline, ready to be picked, or more likely staining the city sidewalks.

Angelica

Arugula

Asparagus

Beets (with tops)

Bok Choy

Cucumbers

Dandelion

Fiddleheads

Garlic Scapes

Green Onions

Haskap

Herbs

Kohlrabi

Lavender

Mulberries

Mushrooms

Mustard Greens

Peas

Radishes (with tops)

Rhubarb

Roses

Salad Mixes

Sorrel

Spinach

Strawberries

String Beans

Swiss Chard

Watercress

Wild Mustard

Summer | July

The sweetest and stickiest month, July is a fruit oasis: blackberries, blueberries, currants, raspberries, the first of the peaches, and, of course, the sweetest moment for strawberries, ripened under the sun and picked before nights are too hot for them to bear. Vegetables like beans and okra grow rapidly, as if they are eager to hop on the grill.

Arugula

Beets (with tops)

Bell Peppers

Blackberries

Blueberries

Carrots (with tops)

Cherries

Cherry Tomatoes

Collard Greens

Cucumbers

Currants

Fennel

Garlic

Green Onions

Herbs

Jalapeños

Kale

Kohlrabi

Lavender

Lettuces

Melons

Mushrooms

Mustard Greens

Okra

Peaches

Peas

Plums

Radishes (with tops)

Raspberries

Salad Mixes

Saskatoon Berries

Snap Peas

Spinach

Strawberries

String Beans

Swiss Chard

Zucchinis

Summer | August

Markets are bursting with summer vegetables and fruits like an over-packed suitcase: artichokes for grilling, sweet corn for nibbling, the tenderest zucchinis (perfect in tacos), fine gold apricots, and blackberries that stain your fingers. Barrels full of an assortment of peppers, and tables laden with collards, chard, and callaloo. Cucumbers sit beside cherries, and grapes are in full swing—as are plums, watermelon, and never to be forgotten, summer tomatoes. This is the apex of the growing season.

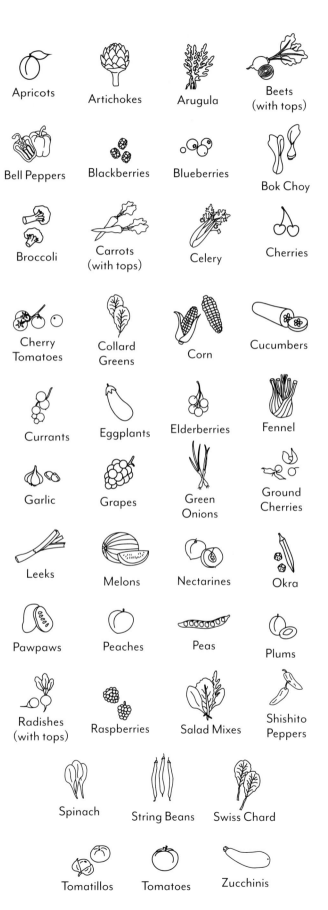

Apricots · Artichokes · Arugula · Beets (with tops)

Bell Peppers · Blackberries · Blueberries · Bok Choy

Broccoli · Carrots (with tops) · Celery · Cherries

Cherry Tomatoes · Collard Greens · Corn · Cucumbers

Currants · Eggplants · Elderberries · Fennel

Garlic · Grapes · Green Onions · Ground Cherries

Leeks · Melons · Nectarines · Okra

Pawpaws · Peaches · Peas · Plums

Radishes (with tops) · Raspberries · Salad Mixes · Shishito Peppers

Spinach · String Beans · Swiss Chard

Tomatillos · Tomatoes · Zucchinis

Fall | September

Not quite summer, not quite fall. This is apple season. This is also peak season for so many vegetables and fruits. Members of the brassica family (broccoli, cauliflower, kale) have been waiting all summer to make their big debut. Summer nightshades like eggplants, peppers, and tomatoes are holding on to the last hot days, and melons spent all summer priming to be at their sweetest.

Apples

Artichokes

Arugula

Beets (with tops)

Bell Peppers

Bok Choy

Broccoli

Broccolini

Carrots (with tops)

Cauliflower

Celery

Cranberries

Cucumbers

Eggplants

Elderberries

Fennel

Garlic

Grapes

Green Onions

Ground Cherries

Hazelnuts

Kale

Leeks

Melons

Mushrooms

Mustard Greens

Peaches

Pears

Peas

Plums

Potatoes

Radishes (with tops)

Rapini

Salad Mixes

Spinach

Sweet Potatoes

Swiss Chard

Tatsoi

Tomatillos

Tomatoes

Zucchinis

Fall | October

Most farmers I talk to rejoice at the word *October*. This is the final big harvest of the year, when all their hard work shows up in the fields, and soon they will have a moment of respite. The brassica family expands to include Brussels sprouts. Sunchokes and sweet potatoes have soaked up enough of the earth's nutrients to get tugged out of the ground, and winter squash like delicata have finally grown up. There are still fruits to be harvested too, like cranberries and Coronation grapes.

Apples

Arugula

Beets (with tops)

Bell Peppers

Broccoli

Brussels Sprouts

Cabbage

Cauliflower

Chestnuts

Chicories

Coronation Grapes

Cranberries

Daikon

Delicata Squash

Elderberries

Fennel

Garlic

Grapes

Horseradish

Kale

Kohlrabi

Leeks

Lettuces

Mushrooms (Maitake)

Mustard Greens

Onions

Parsnips

Pears

Plums

Potatoes

Radishes (with tops)

Rapini

Rutabaga

Spinach

Sunchokes

Sweet Potatoes

Swiss Chard

Tatsoi

Tomatillos

Tomatoes

Turnips

Winter Squash

Fall | November

This is the end of the major harvests. Hardy greens like kale, Swiss chard, and bok choy are still making their way across the fields. Burdock and fall potatoes have sat in the ground so long, they have taken on the flavours of the soil: earthy and pungent and ready to hearten a meal. Neat and interesting broccolis like Romanesco appear in stores and markets, and to avoid getting too over-eager, I like to slowly incorporate a few winter vegetables at a time in my cooking, because I know cabbage and turnips will be a mainstay in the next few months to come.

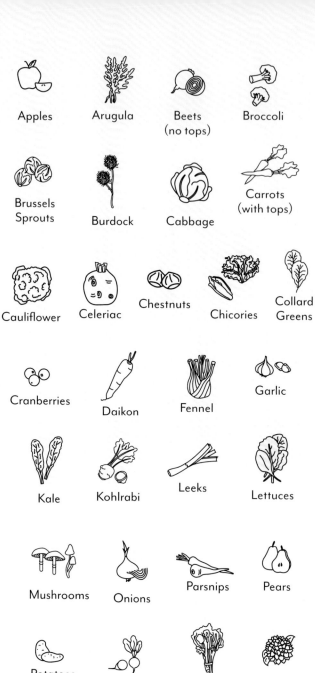

Apples

Arugula

Beets
(no tops)

Broccoli

Brussels
Sprouts

Burdock

Cabbage

Carrots
(with tops)

Cauliflower

Celeriac

Chestnuts

Chicories

Collard
Greens

Cranberries

Daikon

Fennel

Garlic

Kale

Kohlrabi

Leeks

Lettuces

Mushrooms

Onions

Parsnips

Pears

Potatoes

Radishes
(with tops)

Rapini

Romanesco

Rutabaga

Spinach

Sunchokes

Sweet
Potatoes

Swiss
Chard

Tatsoi

Turnips

Winter
Squash

Winter | December

It is official: winter has arrived. Markets are full of provisions like fresh-cut meats, a multitude of cheeses, eggs still laid by hens, and jars of preserves. Winter vegetables, like celeriac and parsnips, are still in their prime despite being harvested mere weeks ago. (That is the beauty of hardy winter vegetables—you can witness many full moons and they'll still be in peak season.) And if it was a particularly warm fall, you may see the final harvests of chestnuts. There are bitter leaves still bearing the frost for us, like red radicchio from the chicory family. Pears, like Bosc and Anjou, harvested in the fall now ripen to peak flavour as the winter endures.

Beets (no tops)

Brussels Sprouts

Burdock

Cabbage

Carrots (no tops)

Cauliflower

Celeriac

Chestnuts

Chicories

Collard Greens

Crab Apples

Cranberries

Daikon

Garlic

Horseradish

Kale

Leeks

Mushrooms (Oyster)

Onions

Parsnips

Pears

Potatoes

Radishes (with tops)

Rapini

Rutabaga

Spinach

Sunchokes

Sweet Potatoes

Swiss Chard

Tatsoi

Turnips

Winter Squash

Winter | January

At the beginning of the year, the fields are all frost and cabbages. When fruit is lacking, beets are sturdy enough to hold their sweetness through this month. So are acorn squashes and Japanese yams, once baked. This is also a month to enjoy gut-loving foods, like soups with fibrous beans and kale, probiotic-rich sauerkraut, and aromatics like garlic and leeks. Winter apples that ripen as they are stored, like Granny Smith and Braeburn, reach their peak flavour in January.

Acorn
Squash

Apples

Beets
(no tops)

Bok Choy

Cabbage

Carrots (no tops)

Celeriac

Chicories

Collard Greens

Garlic

Lacinato Kale

Leeks

Onions

Parsnips

Pears

Potatoes

Rutabaga

Sweet
Potatoes

Swiss Chard

Tatsoi

Turnips

Winter
Squash

Winter | February

When everything else has fled, parsnips, kale, and chicories stay by our side. February is a very cold month. All the more reason to use up your butcher's bones to make an enriching bone broth. It is the aromatics and condiments that can excite the hardy greens like bok choy. I will turn my parsnips into pasta like gnocchi, and find new ways to get excited about Ontario-grown cereal crops, like oats, that warm and sustain.

Beets
(no tops)

Bok Choy

Cabbage

Carrots (no tops)

Celeriac

Chicories

Collard Greens

Garlic

Lacinato Kale

Leeks

Onions

Parsnips

Pears

Potatoes

Rutabaga

Swiss Chard

Tatsoi

Turnips

Winter
Squash

On Ingredients

ONTARIO HARVESTS TELL A STORY of complexities and nuances that will show up in every dish you make. The food that grows here is the foundation of Ontario cuisine. And a good ingredient, one at its peak flavour, can force you to slow down, take pleasure in its smell, feel, taste, and spend hours at the table talking about it—and enjoying a whole meal.

So where can one find these magical ingredients? I believe the best sources are community-supported agriculture (CSA) programs or farmers' markets, though I do not limit myself there. I, too, frequent a few small-scale grocery stores and superstores that carry common fruits and vegetables. If you try to stick to what is in season each month, you will likely get a good, fresh ingredient. If you are unsure, you can always check the label to see if it says "Grown in Ontario" (or your own region). Sometimes, when a store doesn't have what I am looking for, I will implore the store manager to carry it. They will often source the ingredient based on my desperate request. I have made many nice relationships this way and been able to acquire the ingredients I like to use from the shops I frequent most. There is a lot of room to play here, and it is my hope you have as much fun as I do cooking with these foods.

A few spices and other items listed on the following pages and used in my recipes are not grown in Ontario, but that is what happens when you grow up and are influenced by one of the most diverse cities of the world (Toronto). I added them to the book because they are essential components in my home, and most likely in yours. Without them, I would be lost. These ingredients include everyday delights such as lemons, olive oil, salt, sugar, and vanilla. I did my best to cater to what Ontario has to offer, but despite sumac's big role as a local citrus substitute, sometimes you just need a little squeeze of lemon to zhoush things up.

Being tied to local produce or a particular ingredient variety can be ethically nice when you have the resources, but if the best you can afford or find is your local supermarket's brand, please use what you have. Everyone should be able to cook, even if it means not following a recipe exactly. Keep things seasonal, easy, and affordable. When able, stock your pantry with these staples.

Everydays

Eggs

When looking for free-range eggs, it's worth reading the label on the carton carefully. Some producers give a lot of detail about the birds' welfare, feed, and living conditions. All egg recipes in this book were developed with large organic, free-range eggs. Look at the three-digit number to see when the egg was packed (for example 039 means the 39th day of the year: February 8). If you question whether organic eggs taste better, cook a fresh organic egg and a not-so-fresh conventional egg and note the flavour difference. I have yet to be convinced otherwise.

Citrus

Every meal could use brightening. Citrus is one of my favourite ways to do so. It is a multi-purpose fruit; the juice can be used for dressings and sauces, the zest to garnish and enhance, all the while giving your kitchen a pop of colour and refreshing scent. I like to use limes and lemons most of the year, and in the winter, an orange zested and juiced can give a warm feeling to a roasted chicken, and orange marmalade is lovely spread on toast. These are not fruits of Ontario, but what is a taco without a little lime?

Onions

Is a meal really a meal without onions? Caramelized onions—whether they are blond, golden, nutty brown, or cooked low and slow into a jam—sweeten and add a good layer to any dish. Yellow onions and sweet Vidalias are common and available in most grocery stores. I almost think of them as the workhorses of a kitchen, and when the rest of the plants have left us for the winter, onions stand strong beside us. Red onions are my favourite for pickling—the acid brightens them into a beautiful, vibrant pink. I also like to stock up on smaller onions like shallots, pearls, and Cipollinis for mild flavours in dressings or in their full form in pasta dishes.

Garlic

Sometimes when I feel a meal is lacking flavour, it is because I've forgotten to add garlic. I have a farmer friend, Daniel, who specializes in garlic and its many, many varieties. His garlic ranges from mild to hot and the bulbs can have 3 large cloves or 10 small cloves. If you are buying garlic at a farmers' market, you are likely buying a

strong-flavoured garlic, and 1 clove could equate to up to 4 cloves of the average garlic found in most grocery stores. This is where intuitive cooking comes in. You will need to taste and adjust as desired when using fresh garlic varieties like organic Ukrainian or Rose de Lautrec. Daniel has a cheat sheet on his website—thecuttingveg.com—but I am sure any farmer you buy from will have the grower intel on your garlic's pungency.

Salt

The salt I use when cooking is typically kosher salt. The kosher salt called for in the recipes is Diamond Crystal, unless indicated otherwise. Every salt has its own weight and shape, so the measurement of salt will depend on what salt you are using. This is important to recognize not only in my recipes but in any recipe you read. When it comes to seasoning a dish once plated, I like to use a finishing salt like Maldon sea salt, but any flaky salt will work here.

Olive Oil

Like wine, olive oil is complex. It has a multitude of flavours: grassy, buttery, smooth, peppery, and even fruity. I like to have two types of olive oil on hand at all times—and I suggest you do too. The first is a good-quality, full-bodied olive oil for dressings and finishing. I like to buy these in specialty shops where there is a quick turnover of oils. They usually hail from Italy, France, Spain, Greece, or even California. The olives are often pressed the very same day they are picked. The second bottle I have in my kitchen is a cheaper, lighter extra virgin olive oil used for roasting and sautéing. I will always

choose a dark bottle for both types to reduce rancidity, and I buy organic when possible. I like to support the people supporting the land. Olive oil has a smoke point of 405°F (207°C), so for any high-temperature cooking, I opt for another cooking oil (see page 27).

Broth

Used for sipping, steaming, cooking beans, and, of course, for soup. I always like to have broth on hand, especially in the winter. As you can see at the start of the February section (page 248), I enjoy making my own too. It is a great way to use up old kitchen scraps. I prefer broths over bouillon cubes, and if buying, I opt for low-sodium (I like to decide how salty I want my broth). I will choose organic when possible and ideally buy from a butcher that uses up their bones to make broth, but I am no stranger to the Tetra Paks you can get at a grocery store.

Parmesan

The real stuff, not the kind that looks like cardboard shreds in a plastic jar, stored in a cupboard. I am talking about the big wedges with jagged edges and an odour so strong you'd think someone was cooling their smelly feet in your refrigerator. Our brilliant farmers in Ontario age theirs 12 months like a Parmigiano-Reggiano made in the Italian province of Parma, but we call it Parmesan. Parmesan is just as stinky and delicious when made from the cows here.

Nuts & Seeds

It still amazes me to think that Ontario grows a vast amount of nuts and seeds. Hazelnuts in September and chestnuts in October are particular standouts, but hickory nuts, heart nuts, pecans, butternuts, almonds, and even peanuts also grow here. Our province is brimming with sunflowers and pumpkins, so of course a lot of seeds are available too. I love roasting nuts when cooking. I think it changes the flavour of a meal immensely (like the difference between bread and toast). I would suggest never skipping that step. It is nice to get fresh nuts from farmers, usually in the fall, but these nuts are also found at most grocery stores (aside from the heritage hickory nuts, heart nuts, and butternuts, which you have to source from a forager). Nuts are best stored sealed in a jar in the pantry (if shelled) and in the refrigerator (if unshelled).

Fresh Herbs

Tarragon, parsley, cilantro, basil, chives, thyme, oregano, rosemary, mint, bay leaves—need I go on? Fresh herbs can really change a dish. The more I use them, the less concerned I become with what to do with the remaining bouquet I bought. Both soft-stem and woody-stem herbs are used often in my kitchen. No chicken goes roasted without a sprig of something. A salad perks up with mint or basil. I even like to shake things up by adding rosemary to my water. If you do happen to have excess herbs, keep soft-stem herbs, like parsley, in a fresh jar of water, just as you would with flowers, and cover the tops with a damp cloth or plastic bag. Woody-stem herbs, like thyme, can be wrapped in

damp newspaper or tea towel and stored in the refrigerator.

Spices & Dried Herbs

I like to use my spices in their whole form when possible. This is where a good Microplane or mortar and pestle come in handy. If a recipe calls for cinnamon, say, I will use a stick and shave it into its ground state. Ontario grows many herbs and spices—some of my favourite that appear in this book over and over again include sumac, chili, coriander, fennel, dill, tarragon, lavender, oregano, thyme, and mustard seeds. You will also see a lot of freshly cracked black pepper, cardamom, cumin, and cinnamon.

Honey

This is one of my favourite ways to sweeten a dish, thicken a sauce, and bind ingredients, all the while improving my seasonal allergies. The taste of honey comes from the flowers the bees are close to. Every batch you buy will differ. Every neighbourhood in Toronto and every surrounding town has an apiary. I have a friend down the street from me who keeps bees. It is my favourite honey, and I am convinced the product tastes like the honeysuckles lining our street. You can get good honey anywhere; it is often labelled "pure" honey, which means the bees have not been fed corn syrup. Raw honey is a bit creamier and more susceptible to crystallization, though it is best for nutritional purposes. When it comes to incorporating honey into my meals, I like to use unpasteurized. It is heated only slightly to retain its nutritional benefits but enough to preserve its liquid form— easier for drizzling and whisking.

Maple Syrup

I love maple syrup so much. Not just because it adds a caramel sweetness to my pancakes, but because it is Ontario's way of saying "Spring is upon us and all life will resume again." I even share how to tap and make maple syrup in the March section of this book (page 33). In Ontario, we have a lot of sugar maple trees, and why not use them for what they can provide us? A lighter maple syrup has a more delicate flavour in comparison to the robust dark maple. I prefer amber maple syrup for pancakes and cooking. It is the Goldilocks of the maple syrups, but this kind of nuance is completely up to your own taste buds.

Occasionals

Meat & Poultry

All parts of nature deserve respect and thanks when we use them for our own needs. There was a time in Canada when the animals that were eaten were ones that ran wild. Though Canada is still home to many wild animals, the majority of us are eating animals raised on farms. I believe that every animal tells the truth of their life, which is all the more reason not to eat the ones who spent their lives in confinement, but rather were raised on pasture and fed a proper diet. Not everyone has access to well-raised animals, but it is important to me to choose my meats wisely when I can. The recipes that do include meat are distinctly frugal in meat quantities because I would rather eat a good-quality steak on occasion over an average steak often.

them suggest a good option at that particular time of year. They've taught me that there is more to life than salmon, like a good lake trout. I understand not everyone can be so fortunate to have a fishmonger nearby. In that case, shop what is available to you. I recommend hopping on seafoodwatch.org to keep the future of the water viable.

Dairy

When it comes to milk products, organic is a non-negotiable. It takes a lot more work to rely on natural farming methods instead of synthetic pesticides and fertilizers, but cows are treated more fairly and so is the ecosystem. I understand that the price difference between conventional and organic is a hard nut to crack for some, but a little goes a long way with good-quality ingredients. The secret to good cheese, yogurt, butter, or milk begins with the land, and lucky for us, there are many dairy farms and local cheesemakers in this province to choose from. My refrigerator is almost always stocked with butter and Parmesan, sometimes yogurt, but all other dairy constellations are reserved for special occasions.

Pantry Locals

Fish

I like to buy my fish the day I am cooking with it—one day prior at most. This is for freshness but mostly because I do not do well with planning ahead. I frequent a small, very informed fishmonger in my neighbourhood. I try not to show up with an idea in mind, but rather let

Flours

I like to get freshly milled flour from a CSA or a local mill, like k^2 Milling, Anita's Organic Mill, or 1847 Stone Milling here in Ontario. If I am not in a big baking mood, I will buy only in small quantities because I like to use flour while it is fresh, and even the most shelf-stable flours can go rancid quickly. As rustic and wonderful as it is to work with flour out of its paper bag, I find flour is best stored in an airtight glass or plastic container, kept out of direct sunlight in a cool, dry place, like the pantry. Here is a bit more about my favourite flours:

All-Purpose Flour: This is the workhorse of my home baking. It will last a long time stored in the pantry, though it does not clock as much nutritional value as its whole wheat counterpart. That said, the gluten strength and mild flavour makes it great for almost anything, especially cakes, breads, and tarts. I always look for labels that say "unbleached flour." These do not contain preservative chemicals. This type of flour will keep for 6 to 8 months in the pantry.

Whole Wheat Flour: Unlike all-purpose, whole wheat flour includes the wheat germ, bran, and endosperm. This gives baked goods more flavour and density. Store in a sealed container in the pantry and buy only in small batches (unless you're a voracious baker), because it has a relatively short shelf life. This flour will keep for up to 4 months in the pantry.

Red Fife Flour: This is Canada's oldest wheat variety and heritage grain. It is nutty and earthy, and it gives bread, pancakes, and even cookies a savoury depth of flavour. I like to use red fife the same way I would whole wheat, though the gluten in red fife is slower to develop, which results in a soft, tender crumb in things like muffins and cakes. This flour will keep for 4 months in the pantry.

Masa Flour: Where would I be without fresh tortillas? Store-bought taco shells are a crime, and I urge anyone who has not made their own tacos to drop everything and do so now. It is not hard and will forever change how you feel about taco night. All you need is two hands, a few cups of masa, salt, and water. This flour will last for up to 9 months in the pantry.

Dry Edible Beans

Beans have been a staple food in our world for over 10,000 years. They hold a different meaning to everyone. For some, they are scorned as the "poor man's meat." For others, they are praised as healthy sustenance that is easy on this planet. For me, it is a continuation of traditions that make them romantic, exciting, tasty, yet humble and dependable. When dried and stored properly (in airtight glass jars), they are practically indestructible. There are so many beans to choose from, disparate in form and function, but these are my absolute top three that you will always find in my pantry:

Peas: Not technically a bean, peas are quite a linguistic accident, though I like to categorize them in the same world. Dried peas have been an important staple in colder climates (for example, yellow split peas in Quebec). I like peas because they are sweet and adaptable in nearly any meal. Green peas can brighten a winter dish lacking in phytonutrients. Dried peas store well, so my addiction to the garden pea can last all year long.

Kidney Beans: When I think of the epitome of the word *bean*, it's the kidney bean that comes to mind. It is homely, honest, and so ubiquitous. It would be silly of me not to mention that when I speak of the kidney bean, it is not limited to the dense, red kidney bean, but also includes the tender-fleshed white kidney (or cannellini), which is fluffy, mild, and one of my favourites to add sustenance in a delicate salad.

Lentils: The lentil is an ancient sentinel among beans. It is tolerant in even the harshest conditions. Lentils were not always the bean of choice throughout history because of their stronger flavour compared to most other legumes, but I find them earthy, meaty, and slightly nutty. By a perverse reversal of fate, some lentils, like the dark green Le Puy and mini black beluga, became luxury foods. It takes real strength and fortitude to satisfy without using meat, and I find lentils do just that. I love all lentils equally and have a series of them on rotation in my pantry.

Cereal Crops

In my test kitchen, I have an entire shelf of cereal crops: barley, buckwheat, sorghum, spelt berries, rye berries, wheat berries, millet, amaranth, popcorn, and so on. But at home I tend to stick to the three luminaries below, each of which can store for up to 6 months in sealed glass jars. I will rotate through what I have before moving on to a new set, sometimes sprinkling a more peculiar grain, like amaranth or millet, into the mix.

Oats: No matter how bare my cupboard, I'm never without oats. My favourite breakfasts and desserts always seem to include oats, probably because their creamy texture and versatility make them an excellent option to carry any sweet or savoury flavour. Though most oats grown in Ontario are for feed, plenty of small-scale farmers grow oats here and sell them at small local grocers and specialty shops. And with the rise in plant-based diets and alternative milks, there has been a surge of growing opportunities for oats in this province. They technically can last for up to 2 years, but I don't think they have ever overstayed their welcome in my home.

Rice: A well-cooked bowl of rice needs nothing but salt. Most often I will have brown rice for common cooking, white rice almost strictly for Japanese and Korean dishes, and on occasion wild black rice grown in Ontario to pique interest in a bowl of cooked vegetables or sometimes fruit. A note on wild rice: This is Canada's only native cereal. It grows on non-depleted soils within the boreal forest of Ontario.

Wheat Berries: These are the whole wheat kernel (bran, germ, and endosperm) without the husk. They are chewy, nutty, and a nice addition to bulk up a salad that would otherwise be considered an appetizer. Wheat berries seem like they are a specialty crop, but you can find them almost anywhere, including most supermarkets.

Baking Essentials

This is a list of my most frequently used baking items. Not including flours, butter, and natural sweeteners (listed above), these are the ingredients I use most when baking. Almost all of these items can be found at your local supermarket. I like to buy in small sizes to avoid rancidity, and

I choose organic when possible because I like to support those supporting the earth. The only items here that may be hard to find are some of the unsulphured dried fruits. First, unsulphured just means that the fruit is naturally dried without additives. This means your apricots will not be vibrantly orange, but rather a dark brown, as nature intended. These items can most often be found at a bulk shop, and for the eager baker, you can dry them in a dehydrator or in the sun yourself.

- Baking powder (aluminum-free)
- Baking soda
- Pure vanilla extract
- Pure almond extract
- Sugar (granulated and brown)
- Oat milk (from Ontario)
- Dried fruits (from Ontario):
  Apricots, unsulphured
  Mulberries, unsulphured
  Currants, unsulphured
  Apples, unsulphured

Condiments & Seasonings

A condiment can be anything from a spice to a sauce or even a preparation of ingredients to brighten, enhance, and complement the existing flavours in a dish. Condiments are the sidekick that makes everything taste that much better. The Scottie Pippin to Michael Jordan. A bowl of rice (for example) wouldn't be a true dish without a spoonful of one of the items listed below, most of which can be found in any grocery store, and if looking for Ontario produce, I recommend a local specialty store if you have one nearby.

- Ginger (fresh)
- Gochujang
- Grainy mustard (from Ontario)
- Horseradish (fresh)
- Kimchi
- Soy sauce
- Vinegars (from Ontario):
  Apple cider vinegar
  Balsamic vinegar
  Red wine vinegar
  Rice vinegar
  White wine vinegar

Cooking Oils

- Canola oil
- Grapeseed oil
- Sunflower oil
- Vegetable oil

Extras (Not to Be Forgotten)

- Walnut oil
- Capers
- Canned tomatoes
- Cooking alcohol:
  Dry white wine
  Sweet red wine
  Bourbon

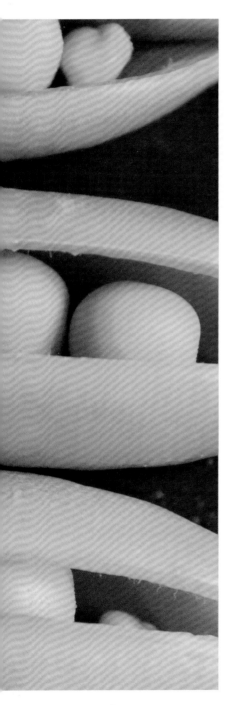

Spring

AS SOON AS THE SAP in the sugar maples begins to rise, everyone in Ontario takes a deep sigh. So long, snow. The emerald-green buds from wild leeks become an epitaph to winter and remind us that there is life again. I'll gladly trade in my toque and parsnips for a windbreaker and scarlet-red rhubarb.

Spring can be confusing at times: Glimpses of bare legs peeking under puffy jackets. Scarves wrapped around tank tops. And the most offensive, socks and sandals. In this awkward transition period, our hopes leap faster than the weather itself. It is a remarkable moment in our kitchens when hardy winter vegetables and young spring buds meet. One day you may be eating butternut squash in Fried Almond Buns with Tarragon Squash Paste (page 35), the next you may be enjoying freshly picked asparagus in Asparagus, Nettle & Dill with Balsamic Glazed Onions on Sourdough (page 69). In the spring, year-round crops like new potatoes and Easter egg radishes are less fibrous and more subtle than their sturdier fall counterparts.

Spring is when we get to benefit from all of winter's conserved energy. Vibrant colours and flavours show up on our plates, like in my Rhubarb, Bay Leaf & Frangipane Galette (page 78) or fern-green Garlic Mushroom Fiddlehead Frittata (page 56). This season is most exciting because these next few months promise something new, something fresh. There's a promise that our days will be brighter, that the sun will return, and that spring's delicate vegetables have emerged.

How To: Tap & Make Maple Syrup

When it finally is 0°C (32°F) and nights still dip below that point, give praise to the high heavens, because the dark, cold winter is over and your sugar maples are ready to tap. The traditional way to collect maple syrup is in a bucket fitted with a spile and nailed to a tree. A healthy sugar maple tree can fill a bucket within a day or so, and at this point you can drink your sap as a sweet water or boil it all down into maple syrup: 5 gallons (20 litres) of sap will convert into 2 cups (500 mL) of syrup. Each batch will change in character depending on when you have tapped your tree. An early season will make a pale and soft syrup, while late-season sap has a deep malty flavour. Keep an eye on nature because the maple syrup season ends as soon as the buds on the twigs begin to open.

Equipment

1 power drill, fitted with a 5/16 drill bit

1 spile, 5/16 in size

1 hammer

1 bucket (2 to 4 gallons/7.5 to 15 litres) with a handle

1 large, heavy pot (3 gallons/11 litres)

Sealable glass jars (I like to use 8-ounce/250 mL jars with wide lids)

2 to 3 coffee filters (for straining syrup into jars; see Note)

Tap a Sugar Maple

Step 1: Scout out a sugar maple tree. To identify that your maple tree is a sugar maple, take a look at the leaves, seeds, and bark. (Note: If you are not on your own property, ask before drilling.)

The leaves:

- Dark green on the outside and light green closer to the centre.
- Each leaf has five segmented lobes—three large, two small—with a smooth U-shape margin between each lobe.
- Leaves are 3 to 5 inches (8 to 12 cm) in both height and width.
- Leaves will grow in sets of two, with one leaf always across from another on every twig.
- On the underside of the leaf, one vein runs through the main lobe, and veins run on two of the smaller lobes on either side.

The seeds:

- The seeds are green with two little wings in the shape of a horseshoe.

The bark:

- Look for a brown, furrowed bark. As a sugar maple ages, the bark changes colour. A young bark is more of a greyish brown, but you do not want to tap a young bark in need of its own sustenance.
- Look for furrowing bark with deep rifts between each plate of bark. The bark will look shaggy from a distance.

Step 2: Measure the diameter of the tree at shoulder height. A sugar maple must be mature enough and at least 10 inches (25 cm) in diameter to be tapped without harming it.

recipe continues

Clean glass jars can preserve syrup safely for up to 1 year, but if you plan to store for longer, it's highly recommended to sterilize your jars in a boiling-hot water bath for 15 minutes to avoid potential bacteria growth and create a heated vacuum seal.

Step 3: Angle your drill slightly upward and drill a hole 2 inches (5 cm) deep into the tree at waist height. Clear away any sawdust.

Step 4: Insert the spile and tap it gently with a hammer for a snug fit. My farmer friend Richard always goes by the "tap, tap, thud" method. Once you hear the thud, your spile is in nice and snug.

Step 5: Hang your bucket on the hook attached to the spile and let the tree drip. Though not mandatory, it is good to have a lid to cover your bucket to keep the hungry little forest creatures at bay.

Step 6: Check your bucket daily for no longer than 3 days (sap left in a bucket for multiple days can spoil). An average maple tree can produce up to 3 gallons (12 litres) of sap per day.

Step 7: Sap can be stored in sealed containers or jars in the refrigerator for up to 7 days, until you're ready to boil it down to syrup. Sap's sugar concentration is relatively low, so you will need to collect quite a bit of sap: 5 gallons (20 litres) of sap will boil down to roughly 2 cups (500 mL) of syrup.

Step 8: Remove the spile with the back of your hammer once you are done collecting sap for the season.

Boil the Maple Sap

Step 9: Turn on your overhead fan to avoid a sticky kitchen (I have been told that boiling sap can evaporate and cling to your kitchen appliances like mud on a shoe, though I have never experienced this in my kitchen. Nor has my maple farmer friend Richard—from By-the-Rock Farm—in his sugar shack). Into a large, heavy pot, pour in the newly collected sap. Bring the sap to a rolling boil and continue to cook, with the lid off, until the sap is golden but not quite syrup consistency yet. Check the temperature with a cooking thermometer. You should reach about 218°F (103°C); this can take anywhere from 90 minutes to 3 hours depending on how much sap you've collected. Let everything rest to cool to room temperature and thicken.

Step 10: Secure a coffee filter on the mouth of each jar (see Note). Gradually ladle your maple syrup into the jars, remove the coffee filter (if you are using one), and seal with a lid. Store maple syrup in the refrigerator for up to 1 year and enjoy on Brioche French Toast (page 43).

Fried Almond Buns with Tarragon Squash Paste

Makes 8 to 12 buns

Jian dui (sesame bun) was first a palace food in the Tang Dynasty of China. It is now a standard pastry in Hong Kong and can be found in most metropolitan cities all over the world. As a teenager growing up in Toronto, I thought dim sum was not complete without one of these sesame-coated, glutinous rice flour buns. When a sweet tooth strikes, I'll forego the dim sum and go straight to my favourite Chinese bakery, Mashion Bakery, specifically for a sesame bun. As they fry, their bellies expand into little pockets encasing a sweet red bean paste.

To celebrate both the Cantonese dessert and Ontario ingredients, this version isn't traditional but rather one inspired by my sweet sesame bun memories. March is known as the "hunger gap" season. This is a time before the first crops of spring appear and there are few vegetables that truly last throughout the winter, squash being one of them. By good fortune, squash is undeniably sweet and nutty and makes for an excellent surrogate to the earthy red bean paste, especially when nested inside a toasty almond-coated pastry. A palace food indeed.

Tarragon Squash Paste

1 cup peeled and cubed butternut squash (1-inch/2.5 cm cubes)

2 teaspoons dried tarragon

1 teaspoon pure vanilla extract

1 tablespoon honey

⅓ cup dried apricots (unsulphured)

⅛ teaspoon kosher salt

Fried Almond Buns

½ cup crushed raw almonds (the size of sesame seeds; see Note)

1⅓ cups (330 mL) water, divided

¾ cup (155 grams) brown sugar

3 cups (390 grams) glutinous rice flour (see Note)

¼ cup (60 mL) Tarragon Squash Paste

6 cups (1.5 litres) sunflower oil, plus more for deep-frying if needed

Make the Tarragon Squash Paste: Preheat the oven to 450°F (230°C) and line a baking sheet with parchment paper. Place the squash cubes on the baking sheet. Roast the squash until golden brown and tender enough that a fork can poke through with ease, 20 to 25 minutes. Set aside to cool.

Once the squash is cool, combine it with the tarragon, vanilla, honey, apricots, and salt in a blender. Blend until a smooth paste has formed. Turn off the blender, remove the lid, and give everything a good stir to ensure the paste is consistently smooth. You will likely have extra paste when making this recipe—for tips on storage and uses, see Note.

Make the Fried Almond Buns: Spread the crushed almonds on a piece of wax or parchment paper and set a small bowl of water beside them.

Boil 1 cup (250 mL) water. Place the brown sugar in a small bowl, and add the boiled water. Whisk with a fork until the sugar has completely dissolved.

recipe continues

The size of the crushed almonds is of most importance in this recipe. To avoid burning, almonds can't be any smaller than the size of a sesame seed. Larger than sunflower seeds and they will not stick. It is a real art to find the balance, but this detail is worth it. A food processor on low speed can be helpful here, but I like to use a chef's knife to ensure I am getting every morsel at an equal sesame-seed-size consistency.

Glutinous rice flour can be found in most grocery stores or online.

Extra tarragon squash paste can be stored in a sealed container in the refrigerator for up to 4 days. It makes for a sweet addition to thicken porridge and/or smoothies.

Place the rice flour in a large mixing bowl. Use a large spoon to make a well in the middle of the bowl, then slowly pour in the dissolved sugar mixture. Stir everything until a sticky, caramel-coloured dough has formed. The consistency will be similar to playdough. If the dough is still too dry, add 1 tablespoon lukewarm water at a time, up to as much as ⅓ cup (80 mL) water, as needed.

Once the dough has formed, pinch off a piece of the dough—roughly the size of a golf ball—and roll it into a ball shape. Repeat with the remaining dough until you have made anywhere between 8 to 12 balls. Hold a ball in the palm of one hand and, with the thumb of your opposite hand, make a deep indent in the centre of the dough. With both hands, pinch the edges of dough with your thumb and index fingers to form a little cup. Repeat with the remaining balls.

Roll 1 teaspoon of the tarragon squash paste into the hollow of each ball. (This may seem like a small amount, but it is enough. Too much paste will stop the ball from sealing.) Shape the dough to cover the paste completely and seal. Continue with the remainder of the dough.

Dip a ball into the small bowl of water (this will help the crushed almonds stick to the ball). Roll the ball over the crushed almonds and set aside on a large plate. Repeat the process with the remaining balls.

Deep-Fry the Buns: Pour the oil into a deep, heavy pot and heat over medium. Make sure there is at least 3 inches (8 cm) of oil in the pot. Use a cooking thermometer to check the heat. Once the temperature reaches 250°F (120°C), use a slotted spoon or spider strainer to add a few balls at a time. (When the balls are in the oil, they may not sizzle right away. That is okay. A few air bubbles are a good sign. This means the oil is not too hot and everything will cook evenly.) Once the almonds have turned golden brown, about 2 minutes, use the back of the slotted spoon to gently press the balls against the side of the pot. Continue applying pressure as the balls expand to about three times their original size, 10 to 12 minutes. Drain the buns on a paper towel–lined plate and continue frying the remaining buns. Serve warm or seal in a container to enjoy later. Fried almond buns will taste delicious for a day or two.

Pickled Carrots with Almond Dukkah

Serves 4

I am always happy when disparate salad ingredients come together without losing their unique qualities. The yogurt is creamy and, when spread across the plate like a cumulus cloud, contrasts nicely with the zip of ribboned pickled carrots and the crunch of my Almond Dukkah. The prep involves pickling carrots, which is surprisingly simple (see page 184), and pounding nuts and spices into a variation of the traditional Egyptian dukkah. I wanted to make the most of the almonds grown in Canada, and they are a very pleasant nutty substitute for what would customarily be sesame seeds. It's not much work to make this, yet it is a bright salad both in its citrusy fresh flavour and aesthetic.

Almond Dukkah

2 tablespoons raw almonds

½ teaspoon ground cumin

½ teaspoon ground coriander

¼ teaspoon kosher salt

¼ teaspoon freshly cracked black pepper

½ cup (125 mL) plain Greek or Balkan-style yogurt

2 cups pickled carrot ribbons (see page 184)

¼ cup fresh mint leaves, roughly chopped

Good-quality extra virgin olive oil, for drizzling

Place the almonds, cumin, coriander, salt, and pepper in a mortar. Use a pestle to grind and pound until the almonds are roughly chopped and everything is well combined. Set the dukkah aside for serving.

To plate the dish, start by scooping a large dollop (about ½ cup/ 125 mL) of yogurt onto a serving plate (the size of the dollop is up to you; there are no rules, really) and use the back of a spoon to spread the yogurt across the plate. Top the yogurt with the pickled carrots. Sprinkle the fresh mint and almond dukkah over the carrots and finish with a drizzle of olive oil.

Jammy Onion Brown Butter Cornbread

Serves a hungry crowd of 8 or 12 with a meal

Cornbread is an ageless culinary baron. It is hardy and nourishing, especially when served alongside a stew on a frigid day—something many of us in Ontario are familiar with in March. The onions are an unexpected savoury twist to a classic dish and one of the vegetables you will see in season all year. This cornbread can stand to be left in the refrigerator for many days to follow—but who knows how long it will really last in your home, so I suggest making two batches and freezing one for later.

¾ cup (180 grams) unsalted butter

½ cup (125 mL) maple syrup

2¼ cups (560 mL) buttermilk

3 eggs

1½ cups (180 grams) medium-grind cornmeal

1 cup (125 grams) all-purpose flour (see Note)

1½ tablespoons baking powder

1½ teaspoons kosher salt

½ teaspoon baking soda

2 onions (any variety will do), peeled and cut into ¼-inch (0.5 cm) rounds

NOTE: *Make this recipe gluten-free by substituting the cornmeal and all-purpose flour with 2½ cups (400 grams) gluten-free cornbread mix. Bob's Red Mill works well as a substitute and includes baking powder in the ingredients. If you use Bob's Red Mill gluten-free cornbread mix, omit the baking powder from the ingredient list too.*

Preheat the oven to 400°F (200°C).

In a 12-inch (30 cm) oven-safe skillet over medium heat, melt the butter. Swirl the pan to give all sides and the bottom of the skillet an even coating. Little bubbles will begin to appear. Continue to cook until the foam subsides and the butter turns a deep nut brown, but keep a close watch to avoid burning. (Brown butter is like a toddler—it thrives with a lot of love but will spontaneously turn on you when you aren't looking. Unlike a toddler, it requires only 6 minutes of your direct responsibility.) Use your nose: a strong scent of caramel butter is the best sign of its readiness.

Pour the brown butter into a large bowl and whisk in the maple syrup and buttermilk. Set the skillet aside; it will be used soon enough. To stop the eggs from cooking before they are whisked into the mixture, dip a finger in the bowl to check that the butter is lukewarm and cool enough to add the eggs; it will take about 5 minutes to cool. Once the eggs have been whisked in, add the cornmeal, flour, baking powder, salt, and baking soda. Whisk until everything is well combined.

Cover the bottom of the skillet (still with butter residue on it) with a layer of fully intact onion rounds. Slowly pour the cornbread batter over the onions; this will stop the onions from rising into the batter. (This is not a huge deal, but for presentation purposes, it is nice to see all the onion swirls at the bottom of the bread.) Place the skillet in the oven and bake until the top is golden brown and the cornbread is cooked through enough to spring back when lightly tapped in the centre, 30 to 40 minutes. Cool in the skillet for 10 minutes before slicing and serving bottom side up, or allow the cornbread to cool completely and store in an airtight container on the counter for up to 3 days or in the freezer for up to 2 months.

Brioche French Toast

Serves 4

Brioche is a sweet French pastry bread enriched with egg and butter, giving it a rich and tender crumb. My favourite French baker, Arnaud, has the best brioche at my neighbourhood market (in Leslieville) on Sundays. On occasion, I like to pick up fresh brioche to enjoy a slice for myself and then serve the rest as a decadent French toast for brunch guests the following day. French toast is an excellent way to repurpose a bread or pastry that may otherwise be considered stale (you can even freeze your loaf and prepare the toast within the next few months). I love submerging the bread in bourbon. It does not make this dish taste boozy but rather brings out its natural sweetness—though, I must admit, I'm guilty of adding even more sweetness by soaking my serving of French toast in maple syrup. March is maple-tapping season and I will ride any excuse to use my fresh syrup. Let this recipe be your hall pass to do the same.

8 eggs, lightly beaten

¼ cup (60 mL) oat milk (or any milk; I prefer the natural sweetness of oats)

3 tablespoons pure maple syrup, plus more for serving

1 tablespoon bourbon (see Note)

2 teaspoons pure vanilla extract

2 teaspoons ground cinnamon

8 slices brioche, about ¾ inch (2 cm) thick

1 tablespoon extra virgin olive oil

2 tablespoons unsalted butter, plus more if needed

Crème fraîche, for serving

In a large mixing bowl, whisk the eggs and milk together. Add the maple syrup, bourbon, vanilla, and cinnamon, and whisk until there are no lumps.

Transfer the egg mixture to a large, deep baking dish. Arrange the slices of brioche in the egg mixture and soak for 20 minutes. Rotate the bread at the 10-minute mark to ensure all slices absorb the egg mixture.

In a large skillet, heat the olive oil over medium. When the oil is warm, add the butter (the combination of these two fats will stop the butter from burning). When the butter begins to bubble, add the slices of brioche to the skillet, as many slices that can fit in an even layer. Cook the brioche until nicely browned on one side, 4 to 5 minutes. Flip it and cook until the second side has browned, 4 to 5 minutes more. Transfer the French toast onto a plate and repeat this process until all toasts are cooked. Add more butter if the skillet begins to look too dry. Serve with maple syrup and a dollop of crème fraîche.

NOTE: *Feel free to omit the bourbon to make this recipe alcohol free.*

Irish Soda Bread

Serves 8 to 12

Like the loaves baked in Irish country homes, this bread is just right for serving at afternoon tea—warm and sliced thick enough to support whatever trimmings you desire. Try with a pat of butter melted by the residual warmth of the bread, or with a spoon (or three) of last night's custard, or toasted and dumped into a bowl of soup where it will slowly sponge up every bit of goodness. The intoxicating smell of fresh bread, akin to fresh ground coffee, in the morning is a pleasant thing most would be happy to wake up to (my hand is raised). An Irish soda bread is a quick (no leaven or yeast necessary) and dense loaf of bread. The baking soda and buttermilk are key to the bread's flavour, texture, and rise. It has a wonderfully crusty exterior and a comforting way about it.

---

2 cups (250 grams) all-purpose flour

2 cups (260 grams) whole wheat flour

1 teaspoon baking soda

4 tablespoons (60 grams) cold unsalted butter, cut into ½-inch (1 cm) dice, plus more for greasing the pan

2 eggs, room temperature

1½ teaspoons kosher salt

1⅔ cups (410 mL) cold buttermilk (see Note)

NOTE: *I have been known to make homemade buttermilk as a quick fix in desperate times for bread. When making your own, any kind of milk works, including non-dairy. Add 1 tablespoon white vinegar to a liquid measuring cup. Add enough cold milk to make 1⅔ cups (410 mL). Whisk together, then let sit for 5 minutes before using.*

Preheat the oven to 400°F (200°C) and generously grease a 5- × 9-inch (12 × 23 cm) loaf pan with butter.

In a large mixing bowl, mix the all-purpose flour, whole wheat flour, and baking soda using a spatula. Use your hands or a pastry cutter to cut the butter into the flour. Mix until the flour feels like coarse crumbs.

In a separate large mixing bowl, whisk the eggs and salt together. Gradually pour in the buttermilk, whisking until blended. Pour the wet ingredients into the dry ingredients and stir gently to moisten the flour—no need to be thorough. Gently fold the dough together until it is too stiff to stir and a thick, spongy dough has formed. Scrape the batter into the pan and push down to cover all four corners of the pan.

Bake until the bread has a firm golden-brown crust that releases easily from the pan, 45 to 55 minutes. Transfer the pan to a wire rack and let it rest for 5 minutes. Run a knife around the edges of the bread before turning the bread out onto a wire rack to cool at room temperature. Serve warm with butter and jam or use to sop up your favourite soups and stews. Leftover bread can be stored at room temperature for up to 2 days. I like to store my soda bread in a linen tea towel, but some people find this way of storing dries the bread out. Storing it in an airtight container works just as well.

How To: Cook with Fiddleheads

Reminiscent of their namesake—the stringed instrument—fiddleheads are a coiled frond of the ostrich fern. You can find fiddleheads in the wet, sunny floodplains of Ontario, though they are available for only 6 weeks of the year. This ephemeral green vegetable captures the fleeting taste of a grassy early spring. If you have never tried a fiddlehead, I can assure you that the flavour is like a love child between asparagus, okra, and a touch of green bean. Sometimes I look at apple trees as a sign of whether fiddleheads are ready. The blossoms of an apple tree signify it is fiddlehead season.

I like to pick the smallest, brightest green fiddleheads of the bunch. The larger, less tightly coiled fiddleheads have a woody texture and much less flavour. If foraging is an option for you, just remember never to take more than 15% of what is in the area; concentrate on harvesting from the centre of the patch to ensure fiddleheads will continue to grow in the future. You can also find fiddleheads at most farmers' markets and local specialty stores between mid-April and late May. I have noticed that some superstores are beginning to carry fiddleheads nowadays too, making them readily available at this time. They are one of the only items in stores that are celebrated as a seasonal delicacy grown wild in our region.

As beautiful as they may be, fiddleheads are susceptible to bacterial contamination. I highly recommend that you boil fresh fiddleheads for 15 minutes or steam them for 20 minutes before eating. Below is a step-by-step guide to preparing this spring green.

Equipment
1 colander
1 medium pot

Fiddleheads
2 cups fiddleheads

Step 1: Sometimes fiddleheads have a papery brown fuzz known as *chaff*. If your fiddleheads have this, begin by removing the chaff from each individual fiddlehead.

Step 2: In a colander, wash the fiddleheads in cold water to remove any residual husk or dirt. Repeat for good measure.

Step 3: Fill a medium pot three-quarters full with water and heat over high. Once boiling, reduce to a dull roar and cook the rinsed fiddleheads for 15 minutes. Drain the fiddleheads in a clean colander and shake the colander to remove any excess water. Rinse the fiddleheads one last time and trim the ends.

Step 4: Proceed with your fiddlehead recipe, like my Garlic Mushroom Fiddlehead Frittata on page 56. I highly recommend using prepared fiddleheads right away. You can dry your fiddleheads, seal them in an airtight container, and freeze for later use, but most of the flavour, texture, and colour will be lost.

Garlic Honey Braised Wild Leeks with Toasted Almonds

Serves 4

We use very few ingredients today that are truly native to Ontario. Wild leeks—ahem, ramps—are one of them. They are a highly anticipated spring plant in Ontario because they are—like fiddleheads—one of the first signs of a new growing season, appearing after a long winter of root vegetables and available only at this time of year (found mostly at farmers' markets, but a few larger grocery stores have started carrying them as they become more popular). Wild leeks grow in the shaded deciduous woods of Ontario and are quite similar to green onions—both pungent and sweet—but wild leeks can be distinguished by their two flat leaves and garlicky aroma. After a day of harvest, I like to cut off the hairy tips, thoroughly scrub out excess dirt, and cook them low and slow to soften into a honey butter. A sprinkle of crunchy almonds goes a long way and makes this dish a really wonderful appetizer.

¼ cup raw almonds, roughly chopped

3 tablespoons unsalted butter

1 clove garlic, minced

1 shallot, peeled and minced

2 tablespoons white wine vinegar

1 tablespoon honey

2 cups (500 mL) water

½ pound (225 grams) wild leeks, hairy ends trimmed (see Note)

Kosher salt and freshly cracked black pepper, to season

In a small dry skillet over low heat, toast the almonds until fragrant, about 5 minutes. Remove from the heat and set aside.

In a large saucepan over medium-high, heat the butter, garlic, shallots, vinegar, honey, and water. Cook, stirring occasionally, until the liquid has reduced by half, 10 to 15 minutes.

Add the wild leeks and cook until wilted, about 2 minutes. Season with salt and pepper. Transfer to a shallow serving bowl. Sprinkle with the toasted almonds and serve.

NOTE

Tips on sustainable harvesting:

- *Harvest only fat-bulbed wild leeks.*
- *Concentrate on the centre of the patch.*
- *Harvest only 15% of the wild leeks to ensure regrowth.*

Crispy Smashed Potatoes with Toasted Coriander Seeds & Bacon Vinaigrette

Serves 4

A meal composed just of potatoes is heaven to me. In fact, that is what this recipe is. A few fluffy clouds cooked in their fine silky coats. And though I'm an advocate for potatoes on their own, there is nothing better to lift the spirit than garlic potatoes roasted until their skins crisp and crackle, drizzled in bacon vinaigrette, and topped with toasted coriander seeds that pop in your mouth. I like to use whatever fresh potatoes are available; new potatoes are a good bet in April. They keep their shape once cooked and if they are colourful, all the better for the eye's appetite.

2 pounds (900 grams) new potatoes (like Purple Majesty or Red Duke of York), scrubbed (see Note)

½ tablespoon kosher salt

¼ cup (60 mL) extra virgin olive oil, divided

Flaky sea salt and freshly cracked black pepper

2 teaspoons coriander seeds

6 strips bacon

2 teaspoons white wine vinegar

2 cloves garlic, minced

¾ cup (180 mL) sour cream, for serving (optional)

NOTE: *There's no need to peel new potatoes—they are perfect just as they are. The tender skins of new potatoes get crispy when parboiled and baked, adding a nice contrast to their fluffy flesh.*

Preheat the oven to 450°F (230°C) and line a baking sheet with parchment paper.

Place the potatoes in a large pot. Add enough water to cover the potatoes and season with the salt. Bring the water to a boil. Once boiling, immediately reduce the heat to medium-low. Simmer the potatoes until they can be easily pierced with a fork, about 15 minutes (time will vary depending on the size of your potatoes; be careful not to overcook, as they'll fall apart when smashed). Drain and transfer the potatoes to the prepared baking sheet. Let cool slightly.

Place another baking sheet on top of the potatoes. Push down firmly to smash the potatoes. Drizzle 2 tablespoons olive oil over the potatoes. Season with flaky sea salt and pepper. Roast the potatoes until crispy and golden brown, 35 to 40 minutes.

Meanwhile, in a dry skillet over medium heat, toast the coriander seeds in a dry skillet over medium heat. Heat until they begin to pop, 2 to 3 minutes. Remove from the heat and set aside for serving.

Cook the bacon in the same skillet. Begin by placing the bacon evenly across the skillet and turning the heat to medium-low. Flip the bacon when it begins to curl and continue to cook, flipping every so often, until very crisp, about 10 minutes. Reserve the fat for the dressing. Place the bacon on a paper towel and crumble into small pieces for serving. Transfer the bacon and bacon fat to a small bowl. Mix in the remaining 2 tablespoons olive oil, vinegar, and garlic. Whisk to combine and season with kosher salt.

Use the back of a spoon to evenly spread the sour cream across a large plate. Top with crispy smashed potatoes. Spoon the bacon vinaigrette over the potatoes. Scatter with toasted coriander seeds and serve.

Mustard-Crusted Rack of Lamb with Fresh Mint Sauce

Serves 4

A rack of lamb makes for a beautiful centrepiece at the dinner table and though simple to make, in my home it is reserved for special occasions—a true meal for the romantics. With a little care (pre-rub and appreciation) and 20 minutes you will have a tender pink centre that deepens into a warm brown exterior. Lamb is at its best cooked with a grainy mustard—the grainier the better—and even more so when fragrant herbs like mint are made into an extraordinarily refreshing sauce to complement the meal.

Mustard-Crusted Rack of Lamb

1 clove garlic, minced

⅓ cup (80 mL) grainy mustard

3 sprigs fresh thyme, roughly chopped

2 tablespoons extra virgin olive oil

Flaky sea salt and freshly cracked black pepper

2 (4-rib) racks lamb (each 1 pound/450 grams; see Note)

Fresh Mint Sauce

1 cup fresh mint, plus a few extra sprigs of mint for serving

1 shallot, peeled and minced (about ½ cup)

1 teaspoon flaky sea salt

2 teaspoons fennel seeds

1 teaspoon ground sumac

½ cup (125 mL) extra virgin olive oil

¼ cup (60 mL) white wine vinegar

Preheat the oven to 425°F (220°C).

With a mortar and pestle, grind the garlic, mustard, and thyme. Add in the olive oil and muddle to form a paste. Season with salt and pepper. Arrange the lamb racks facing each other, bone ends up and tipped toward one another on a large plate or baking sheet. Rub the garlic mustard mixture over the lamb to season liberally.

Shake the lamb of excess garlic mustard rub, then place the lamb in a 9- × 13-inch (23 × 33 cm) roasting pan and loosely intertwine the bones. Roast until the centre of the meat reaches 130°F (54°C) on an instant-read thermometer for medium rare, about 20 to 25 minutes. Transfer the lamb to a platter and tent with foil.

While the lamb is roasting, finely chop the mint. Add the shallots, 1 teaspoon salt, fennel seeds, and mint to a mortar. Muddle with the pestle until all the ingredients are well ground. Add the sumac, oil, and vinegar and continue to grind until a pesto-like sauce has formed. Alternatively, a small food processor will work just as well. Give the first set of ingredients a good 8 to 10 pulses before adding the sumac, oil, and vinegar. Pulse 10 more times. Set the mint sauce aside for serving.

Slice the lamb only when you are ready to serve. Garnish with mint sprigs and serve the mint sauce alongside.

NOTES

On buying lamb: It helps to buy lamb that was well raised—they are more tender based on their intra-muscular fat composition. Whatever lamb you choose, pick one with a thin layer of fat that appears waxy (not dull or slimy).

Make plenty more mint sauce than you need because it can last for up to 2 weeks in the refrigerator and tastes wonderful drizzled over a salad or tossed with grains, like millet.

Savoury Wild Leek Crepes with Gooey Mozzarella

Serves 4

I find crepes to be a perfect blank canvas for highlighting any ingredient your heart desires, from sweet fruits to savoury greens. Might I suggest using this kind of ingredient freedom to your advantage and cook with what is in season? In this case, with Ontario's ephemeral green: wild leeks (ramps)—the first greens to appear after a long winter. You will know when they are ready to harvest the moment you see a Toronto pedestrian wearing shorts with a winter jacket on a balmy April day. Their green leaves and onion-like bulbs need nothing more than some soft, chewy mozzarella melting inside.

1 cup (125 grams) all-purpose flour

½ teaspoon kosher salt, plus more to season

2 eggs

⅔ cup (160 mL) 2% milk, plus more if needed

2 tablespoons unsalted butter, melted

2 tablespoons extra virgin olive oil, divided

2 cloves garlic, minced

1 bunch wild leeks (6 to 8 leeks), hairy ends trimmed

½ cup (1½ ounces/40 grams) shredded mozzarella

NOTE: *Crepes are a serve-as-you-make kind of dish. No need to be polite and wait for everyone to have their meal; it is all part of the experience. The one who gets the short stick eats last. And dare I say they are the luckiest of the lot because, by now the cook has mastered the art of crepe making.*

In a large mixing bowl, combine the flour and salt until well mixed. Add the eggs, milk, and butter and whisk together to form a wet batter. Set the batter aside for 30 minutes to rest. Once rested, give the batter a stir—the consistency should be similar to heavy cream. If it seems too thick, add a little more milk, 1 teaspoon at a time, stirring as you add.

Heat a large skillet over medium and coat with 1 tablespoon oil. Once the skillet is hot, add the garlic and sauté until fragrant, 2 minutes. Add the leeks. Cook until the leeks have wilted, 4 to 5 minutes. Remove the leek mixture from the skillet and set aside.

Wash the skillet and place back on the burner over medium heat. Lightly coat the skillet with the remaining 1 tablespoon oil. Once the skillet is hot enough (you can test this by flicking a droplet of water into the pan—if it sizzles, you are good to start cooking), add a quarter of the batter. Holding the handle, give the skillet a swirl to spread the batter to a thin even round. Cook for 30 seconds. Use a firm spatula to flip the crepe. Place a quarter of the garlic-infused wild leeks and cheese across the centre of the crepe. Continue to cook for another 30 seconds. Turn off the burner, fold the crepe, and allow it to sit in the skillet for another 30 seconds to melt the cheese and let the crepe crisp up a little more before removing to serve. Repeat with the remaining crepe batter and fillings—there will be enough for three more.

Garlic Mushroom Fiddlehead Frittata

Serves 4 to 6

Fiddleheads are a treasured Ontario green. They are as old as dinosaurs and available for only 4 of the 52 weeks in a year. I love hosting a brunch this time of year and making a frittata featuring these little emerald swirls, which can be a bit of a novelty for those guests who have never tried them before. In this dish, the fiddleheads are nestled with fresh herbs and savoury mushrooms in a bed of creamy eggs and melty cheese. You can serve the frittata in the very skillet it is cooked in, making this a one-dish meal— something to be desired indeed.

1 tablespoon extra virgin olive oil

2 yellow onions, peeled and thinly sliced

2 cloves garlic, minced

½ cup roughly chopped shiitake or porcini mushrooms

1 cup cooked fiddleheads (see page 46 and Note)

Kosher salt and freshly cracked black pepper, to season

2 sprigs fresh thyme, leaves only

6 eggs, beaten with a pinch of kosher salt

1½ tablespoons whole milk (alternative milks will work here too)

4 ounces (110 grams) feta, crumbled

Preheat the oven to broil on high.

In a large oven-safe skillet (ideally cast iron), heat the olive oil over medium. Add the onions and sauté. Give the onions an occasional stir to get everything equally caramelized, sticky, and golden brown, about 15 minutes. Add the garlic and mushrooms. Sauté everything until fragrant and the mushrooms are tender, about 5 minutes. Add the prepared fiddleheads, salt, and pepper. Cook 2 to 3 more minutes until everything is tender but not mushy. Turn off the heat and stir in the thyme.

In a large bowl, whisk the beaten eggs and milk together. Mix in the crumbled feta and the fiddlehead mushroom mixture and stir until everything is evenly distributed. Pour the egg and vegetable mixture back into the oven-safe skillet. Cook on the stovetop over medium-low until the eggs begin to set, about 10 minutes. Finish cooking the frittata under the broiler until the top of the frittata has light brown leopard spots across it and the cheese has melted nicely into the set eggs, 3 to 5 minutes. Let cool for 5 minutes before serving. Extras can be covered in an airtight container and stored in the refrigerator to be heated and enjoyed the next day.

NOTE: *To avoid mushy fiddleheads in this dish, I like to boil the fiddle-heads for only 10 minutes, as opposed to 15, knowing that they will continue to cook in the frittata.*

How to: Bake an Almond Bourbon Babka

Serves a crowd

This babka presents itself under the guise of a humble dessert, but when cut into, it is fluffy, flaky, and delightfully marbled with an almond bourbon filling. Something you may not consider an Ontario ingredient, almond trees are quite hardy, are susceptible to frost, and do indeed grow in Ontario. Their spring blossoms are much like cherry blossoms, and when the almond is ready, a little green fruit splits down the centre, exposing an almond shell. I've added bourbon—just a wee bit—to bring out the babka's almond flavour; it is not immediately apparent, but the addition lends a deep, mellow fruitiness, intensifying the almond flavour. When I bake this for my family, they tend to devour half of the dessert in a matter of minutes, and the remainder is usually enjoyed the next day with a milky tea so no one could accuse us of having cake for breakfast (although no judgement if you choose to do so).

Equipment

2 small mixing bowls

1 medium mixing bowl

1 large mixing bowl

1 clean tea towel

1 rolling pin

1 parchment-lined baking sheet

Almond Bourbon Filling

½ cup (125 mL) pure maple syrup

⅓ cup (80 mL) creamy natural almond butter

¼ cup (60 grams) unsalted butter, melted and cooled slightly

2 teaspoons ground cinnamon

½ teaspoon pure almond extract

⅛ teaspoon kosher salt

1½ tablespoons bourbon

Make the Almond Bourbon Filling

Step 1: In a small mixing bowl, whisk together the maple syrup, almond butter, butter, cinnamon, almond extract, salt, and bourbon. The filling will first appear watery like an icing glaze, but as the butter cools, it will become thicker like molasses. Store the filling in the refrigerator to thicken while preparing the dough.

Make the Babka Dough

Step 2: In a medium mixing bowl, mix the yeast with the lukewarm water and 1 tablespoon sugar. Set aside for 10 minutes, until bubbles begin to form. Once the yeast has confirmed it is alive (with the bubbles), whisk in the milk, egg yolks, vanilla, and almond extract.

Step 3: In a large mixing bowl, use a wooden spoon to combine the flour, the remaining ¼ cup (50 grams) sugar, and salt. Once all the dry ingredients are well combined, slowly pour in the milk mixture and continue to mix for 2 to 3 minutes, until a dough has formed. Add the butter, one piece at a time, and begin to knead the dough with your hands as you incorporate all of the butter. Continue until you have a smooth ball, 10 to 12 minutes. (The dough may seem crumbly at first, but don't worry, just continue to knead. The butter will incorporate well and a ball will form nicely.)

recipe continues

Babka Dough

½ tablespoon (4 grams) instant dry yeast

1 tablespoon lukewarm water

¼ cup (50 grams) + 1 tablespoon granulated sugar, divided

½ cup (125 mL) oat milk (or any milk; I like the natural sweetness of oat milk)

2 egg yolks

½ teaspoon pure vanilla extract

½ teaspoon pure almond extract

2½ cups (325 grams) "00" flour, plus more for dusting

½ teaspoon kosher salt

½ cup (120 grams) unsalted butter, cut into 8 pieces, room temperature

To Finish

1 egg yolk

1 tablespoon oat milk (or any milk)

1 tablespoon powdered sugar (optional)

Step 4: Cover the dough in the mixing bowl with a tea towel and set aside on the counter for 1 hour. The dough will rise slightly. Place the bowl in the refrigerator for another hour until the dough is firm and has doubled in size.

Step 5: Once the dough has doubled in size, halve the dough into two portions. On a lightly floured surface, roll each ball of dough into an 8- × 10-inch (20 × 25 cm) rectangle. Spread half the almond bourbon filling over each rectangle of dough, but leave a ½-inch (1 cm) border around the edges.

Step 6: Starting with the long side closest to you, begin to roll a rectangular dough lengthwise away from you to form a long log. Cut the log in half lengthwise. With the cuts facing up, gently plait pieces over each other, making a two-strand braid. Set the braid aside and repeat with the second rectangle of dough.

Finish the Babka

Step 7: Preheat the oven to 375°F (190°C) and line a baking sheet with parchment paper. Gently transfer the two braids of babka to the prepared baking sheet and press the ends together to form one large circle.

Step 8: In a small mixing bowl, whisk together the egg yolk and oat milk. Use a pastry brush to glaze the babka with the milk mixture.

Step 9: Bake the babka on the centre rack of the oven until a skewer inserted into the centre of the dough comes out clean and all of the exposed almond bourbon swirls are firm to the touch, 40 to 45 minutes. Set the babka on a cooling rack to cool completely—and there is always an option to dust the babka with powdered sugar just before serving.

Mushroom Garlic Pot-Stickers

Makes 18 to 20 pot-stickers

The story of how pot-stickers came to be is an endearing one: they were "invented" by accident by a chef in China's Imperial Court when he burnt a batch of dumplings after leaving them on the stove too long. The result was a golden sunset–coloured crust, so crispy the crunch reverberated around the table. I am thankful to the chef for that happy accident because they have been far and away my favourite post-karaoke-night snack on the neon-lit strip of Spadina Avenue since I was old enough to diabolically sing at a bar. As I get older, I prefer the stroll in my neighbourhood to my favourite dumpling spot—Dumpling House—to get their fried dumplings. These pot-stickers have a delicious vegetarian filling that highlights the umami magic of this season's portobello mushroom.

Pot-Sticker Dough

1½ cups (190 grams) all-purpose flour

Pinch of kosher salt

½ cup (125 mL) hot water

Mushroom Garlic Filling

1 tablespoon canola oil

1 teaspoon minced fresh ginger

1 clove garlic, minced

3 cloves black garlic, minced (see Note)

1¼ cups finely diced napa cabbage

Fine sea salt and freshly cracked black pepper

2 cups finely diced portobello mushrooms

3 green onions, hairy stems removed and finely diced

1 tablespoon tamari

1 tablespoon sesame oil

Dipping Sauce

2 tablespoons rice vinegar

2 tablespoons tamari

Make the Pot-Sticker Dough: In a large mixing bowl, combine the flour and salt. Slowly pour in the hot water. Use chopsticks or a fork to whisk the flour mixture until a crumbly dough has formed. Shape the dough into one large mass and turn out onto a lightly floured work surface. Knead into a smooth ball, about 10 minutes. Sprinkle the dough with flour, cover loosely with plastic wrap, and set aside for 1 hour. After the dough has rested, unwrap and knead again for 5 minutes. Cover once more with plastic wrap and set aside for 30 minutes more.

Make the Mushroom Garlic Filling: In a large skillet over medium-high heat, warm the canola oil until the surface shimmers, then add the ginger, garlic, black garlic, and cabbage, followed by a generous seasoning of salt and pepper. Continue to stir until the cabbage begins to wilt, 5 to 6 minutes. Add the mushrooms, green onions, tamari, and sesame oil. Continue to cook until there is only a little liquid left in the skillet and the mushrooms are a glossy nut brown, 6 to 8 minutes. Remove from the heat and set aside.

Make the Dipping Sauce: In a small mixing bowl, whisk together the rice vinegar and tamari. Set aside for serving.

recipe continues

To Cook

1 tablespoon canola oil

1 tablespoon sesame oil

1 cup (250 mL) water, divided

Make the Pot-Stickers: Divide the dough into eight pieces. On a floured work surface, roll each piece into an 8-inch (20 cm) long rope. Cut each rope into four pieces (each 1½ ounces/40 grams) and roll into balls, then sprinkle the balls with flour. Use a rolling pin to roll out each ball into a 3½-inch (9 cm) round. Spoon 2 teaspoons of the filling into the centre of each round. Fold the round like a taco and pinch the sides together. Once sealed, use your thumb and index finger to squeeze and pleat the edges four to five times to help seal in the filling.

Cook the Pot-Stickers: Heat a large skillet over medium-high and lightly coat the bottom with the canola and sesame oils. Place 9 to 10 pot-stickers in the skillet at a time, flat side down, to form a tight circle, with each pot-sticker's bottom fully kissing the pan. Allow the pot-stickers to sizzle in the skillet for 2 to 3 minutes before adding ½ cup (125 mL) water. Cover with a lid immediately and reduce heat to medium-low. Cook until the liquid inside the skillet is boiling (if you are not using a clear lid, you may need to listen for a rumble or take a quick peek to see), 10 to 12 minutes. Remove the lid and increase heat to medium-high. Allow the water to boil off and the bottoms of the pot-stickers to brown, about 5 minutes. Gently unstick the pot-stickers with a spatula and transfer to a plate, bottom side up. Repeat with the remaining pot-stickers and ½ cup (125 mL) water. Serve with the dipping sauce.

NOTE: *Black garlic is a type of garlic slow-roasted until it becomes black and robust, like sweet and umami-rich mushrooms. You can find black garlic at most farmers' markets and Korean and Chinese grocery stores.*

Snap Pea & Asparagus Garlic Broth

Serves 4

This seems like a simple soup, but it's one of many flavours and for me, enough to stave off any spring flus knocking on your door. To lay the flavour foundation for this soup, plunge an entire head of garlic into water to start. The asparagus and snap peas fine-tune the robust garlic broth—their sweet and fresh bites are crisp little nibbles in an otherwise very grounding soup. I have decided that a sprig of fresh thyme is a happy herb to add, then fished out at the last minute before serving.

1 bunch asparagus

4 cups (1 litre) water

1 head garlic, cloves separated and peeled

1 sprig fresh thyme

Kosher salt, to season

1 cup roughly chopped snap peas

½ cup roughly chopped chives (if chives came with blossoms, reserve and use as garnish)

Good-quality extra virgin olive oil, for drizzling

Flaky sea salt and freshly cracked black pepper, to season

A few thick slices toasted sourdough, for serving (optional)

Snap off the woody ends of the asparagus and discard. Cut the asparagus spears into 1-inch (2.5 cm) pieces, keeping the blossoming tops intact.

Heat a large pot over high. Add the water and garlic cloves and bring to a boil. Once the garlic broth is at a mad boil and looks ready to hop from the pot, reduce heat to medium-low, add the thyme, and season with salt. Simmer, partially covered, until the garlic begins to soften to fork-tender, about 30 minutes. Remove the thyme sprig (thyme leaves can be left in the broth).

Purée the broth with an immersion blender. The soup will be smooth but still thin. Add the asparagus, snap peas, and chives. Continue to cook over medium-low until the asparagus and peas soften, 6 to 8 minutes.

Remove the soup from the heat. Finish with a drizzle of olive oil and a sprinkling of sea salt and pepper, if desired, and garnish with chive blossoms (if you have them). Bring the soup to the table and serve with thick slices of toasted sourdough brushed with olive oil and rubbed with cut raw garlic, if you like.

Roasted Ruby Radish on Herbed Torn Greens

Serves 2

When I visit markets this time of year, I find the overflowing baskets of ruby-red radishes impossible to ignore. Too pungent for me when raw, they become sweeter and distinctively earthy when roasted. And best of all, not a single part of a radish—from its leaves to its roots—goes unused, as you'll see in this dish: the leaves are torn into the salad and the roots are roasted. And while you may want to toss the scarred unused bits, they too can be frozen and used to zhoush up a future soup stock. If your radishes do not have green tops, now is a good time to try out any of the 50 children in the bitter greens family. Some of my favourites are tatsoi, angelica, mustard, and dandelion. There is something very endearing to me about a simple recipe that is purposely imperfect. I find a lot of joy and comfort in easy salads like this one—it's spectacular on its own, but also makes a great companion to a nice fish or, even better, the Mustard-Crusted Rack of Lamb (page 52).

½ cup quartered ruby-red radishes (known as Cherry Belle radishes)

4 tablespoons extra virgin olive oil (or duck fat if you are feeling saucy), divided

Kosher salt, to season

2 cloves garlic, minced

Juice of ½ lemon (about 2 tablespoons)

2 teaspoons honey

3 cups mixed fresh bitter greens (I like mustard, dandelion, radish tops, lamb's quarters, komatsuna, angelica, or tatsoi)

¼ cup roughly torn fresh mint leaves

Flaky sea salt, to season

Preheat the oven to 375°F (190°C) and line a baking sheet with parchment paper.

In a large mixing bowl, toss the radishes with 1 tablespoon olive oil and a pinch of kosher salt. Place the radishes on the prepared baking sheet and roast until fork-tender and a shiny, golden brown, about 25 minutes. Set aside until ready to plate.

In a small mixing bowl, whisk together the remaining 3 tablespoons olive oil, garlic, lemon juice, honey, and a pinch of kosher salt. Set aside for serving.

Use your hands to gently tear the bitter greens into bite-size pieces and plate them. Drizzle the dressing over the plated greens. Top with the mint and roasted radishes and sprinkle with flaky sea salt to season.

Asparagus, Nettle & Dill with Balsamic Glazed Onions on Sourdough
Serves 4

Some of the first greens of the year appear in May—asparagus being one of the most popular of the lot, and for good reason. When asparagus is in peak season they are vibrantly green with tender tips that are never mushy but, rather, firm and tight. As for their flavour, whether you are on team thick or team thin, choose your own journey because the size will not matter. The important thing here is that peak-season asparagus are less bitter and much sweeter than their off-season counterparts. All the better to eat with jammy onions, buttery nettles (another spring green), and a vivacious punch of dill on top of soft sourdough.

---

1 tablespoon extra virgin olive oil

4 tablespoons (60 grams) unsalted butter, room temperature, divided

2 Vidalia onions (about 1 pound/ 450 grams), thinly sliced

Kosher salt, to season

2 tablespoons balsamic vinegar

2 cups nettle leaves, handled with care (see Note)

1 pound (450 grams) asparagus, woody ends snapped off

4 slices fresh sourdough, ½ inch (1 cm) thick

1 handful fresh dill, stems removed and roughly chopped

¼ cup Farmer's Cheese or Fresh Ricotta (page 115)

Flaky sea salt and freshly cracked black pepper, to season

Good-quality extra virgin olive oil, for drizzling

NOTE: *Raw nettles can sting when handled, so be sure to wear gloves or use tongs when you cook with them. As soon as they are blanched, they lose their stinging qualities.*

In a large skillet over medium, heat the oil until the surface shimmers, then add 2 tablespoons butter (the combination of these two fats will stop the butter from burning). When the butter begins to bubble, reduce heat to medium-low and stir in the onions. To get a rich caramelized flavour, keep the heat at medium-low for 15 to 20 minutes, giving the onions an occasional stir. Reduce heat to low and add a pinch of salt and the vinegar to deglaze the skillet. Continue to cook until the onions turn golden brown and are jammy and sticky like caramel, about 5 minutes. Transfer to a bowl and set aside.

Fill a medium mixing bowl with water and a couple of cubes of ice, and set aside. Heat a large pot of water and season with salt. Once the water comes to a rolling boil, use tongs or gloves to place the nettles into the water. Cook for 1 minute only before shocking them in the ice bath. Drain the nettles in a colander and set aside to dry.

In a large skillet over medium-low heat, melt the remaining 2 tablespoons butter. Add as much asparagus as fits in the skillet without overcrowding (this will depend on the size of your asparagus) and cook, flipping every so often, until tender, about 7 minutes per side. Remove the asparagus from the heat and set aside. Repeat with the remaining asparagus. While the asparagus is cooking, toast the sourdough.

Plate each dish with one piece of toast, then top with a handful of nettles, a quarter of the onions, and five or six asparagus spears. Sprinkle each toast with dill and crumbled farmer's cheese. Season with salt and pepper and drizzle with olive oil before serving.

King Oyster Mushroom "Scallops" & Roasted Turnips on Minty Fava Bean Mash

Serves 4

Turnip and I have a complicated history. When I was a child, my mother's "Irish cooking" style was to boil vegetables for so long, they reached that perfect trifecta of mushy-sour-watery. But I have matured since the days of overcooked vegetables and am a woman of second chances. When my farmer friend Liz gifted me a bouquet of Hakurei turnips—smooth ivory white and slightly smaller than the blush-shouldered turnips you normally see at the store—I decided to give them another go. I salted and seared them in oil, and what came out was a sweet, nutty, and slightly starchy delight. Just like that, my turnip tribulations washed away. After voraciously testing recipes, I found matching them with late-spring essentials like mint, basil, and fava beans to be an unparalleled combination. The buttery delight of the mushroom "scallops," the light herby mash, and of course the dichotomous bittersweet turnip may seem to be at odds with one another, but they blend together into a brilliance of textures, colours, and flavours.

---

8 very small (golf-ball-size) turnips, trimmed (or 4 small turnips, trimmed and quartered)

2 cups fava beans, pods removed and cooked (or canned, then strained and rinsed)

1 loose cup basil leaves (about 1 bunch)

1 loose cup mint leaves (about 1 bunch)

1 tablespoon white wine vinegar

Pinch of kosher salt, plus more to season

1 tablespoon extra virgin olive oil

1 cup (240 grams) king oyster mushrooms, scrubbed and cut into ½-inch (1 cm) rounds

Good-quality extra virgin olive oil, for drizzling

Freshly cracked black pepper, to season

In a large pot over high heat, bring 6 cups (1.5 litres) lightly salted water to a boil. Once the water has reached a dull roar, reduce heat to medium and add the turnips. Cook until the turnips are fork-tender, 15 to 20 minutes (this will depend on the size of your turnips).

In the meantime, in a large, sturdy mixing bowl, combine the beans, basil, and mint. Use a potato masher or a fork to smash the beans into the fresh herbs. Once everything has been well incorporated and the beans are fully mashed, pour in the vinegar and season with a generous pinch of salt. Give everything one more quick mash and set aside to serve.

Once cooked, strain the turnips. Heat a large skillet over medium and add 1 tablespoon olive oil. Once the oil is hot, fry the sliced mushrooms and turnips until golden brown and crisp on the side kissing the skillet, about 4 minutes. Flip and cook for another 4 to 5 minutes, until the second side is also golden brown. Remove both the turnips and mushrooms from the skillet and set aside for serving.

Divide the minty fava bean mash among four plates. Top with the king oyster mushroom "scallops" and place a few turnips in the centre of the mash. Drizzle with olive oil and season with salt and pepper before serving.

Prince Apple Elk Burgers
Serves 8

Elk is much leaner than beef, although I wouldn't consider it so lean that it tastes gamey. Nonetheless, beef is an easy substitute if you do not have access to ground elk (though most butcher shops and some farmers at the market will have elk). Peak-season ingredients, namely celery and green onions, are added to the burgers along with basil, apples, and capers to bolster the meat's umami flavours but not overpower. Together they form a moist symphony of fresh, sweet, and briny reinforcement to possibly the first barbecue meal of the season. There is a lot of flavour involved, so I wouldn't suggest too many toppings here. The Roasted Ruby Radish on Herbed Torn Greens (page 66) or Peach, Burrata & Basil Salad (page 102) would make nice side options.

1 tablespoon extra virgin olive oil

½ cup finely chopped green onions

2 Prince apples (or Granny Smith or other tart apples), peeled, cored, and diced

½ cup finely chopped celery

4 pounds (1.8 kilograms) ground elk (or beef)

¼ cup capers

1 tablespoon caper brine

½ teaspoon fine sea salt

¼ teaspoon freshly cracked black pepper

2 teaspoons hot sauce

½ cup finely chopped basil leaves

8 fresh buns, sliced in half

In a large skillet over medium, heat the oil. Add the green onions, apples, and celery and sauté until tender, 8 to 10 minutes. Set aside to cool for 10 minutes before handling.

Once cool, add the sautéed mixture to a large bowl with the elk, capers, caper brine, salt, pepper, hot sauce, and basil. Use your hands to shape the burger into eight patties. Place the patties on a plate, cover, and refrigerate for up to 2 hours.

When ready to cook, lightly oil a grill and preheat to medium-high. Grill the patties until cooked through (an internal temperature of 140°F/60°C on an instant-read thermometer), about 7 minutes per side. Let the burgers rest for 5 minutes before serving. Meanwhile, toast the buns on the grill. Serve the burgers on the toasted buns.

NOTE: *I like to keep things simple and top my burgers with extra-grainy mustard and microgreens, but these are now your burgers, so top with what you fancy.*

Chickadee Carrot Cake with Ground Cherry Custard

Makes one 3-layer, 8-inch (20 cm) cake

This may be the best cake I have ever made, and it's a special nod to one of Ontario's year-round residents, the black-capped chickadee who also enjoys a dish made with an array of nuts. This also may be the longest ingredient list in the book, but I promise that all the steps and ingredients will make a cake that you'll swoon for. This cake is an opportunity to use the first round of ground cherries of the season. Bright-yellow Southern Ontario fruits pleasantly encased in tan paper husks, ground cherries are tart, and little, and pop in your mouth like a grape tomato. But most importantly, they make the tastiest custard for desserts.

Ground Cherry Custard

¼ cup ground cherries, plus more for topping (see Note)

4 egg yolks (see Note)

⅔ cup (135 grams) granulated sugar

⅛ teaspoon kosher salt

6 tablespoons (90 grams) unsalted butter, room temperature

Cake

2 cups gluten-free flour blend with xanthan gum (see Note)

2 teaspoons baking powder

2 teaspoons baking soda

1 teaspoon kosher salt

3½ cups coarsely shredded carrots

1 cup blanched sliced almonds, plus more for topping

½ cup plump dried apricots, soaked in lukewarm water for 30 minutes then roughly chopped (see Note)

1 cup chopped walnuts, plus more for topping

1½ cups (300 grams) granulated sugar

1 cup (250 mL) canola oil

4 eggs

Make the Ground Cherry Custard: Fill a medium pot midway with water and set it to boil. While waiting for the water to boil, place the ground cherries, egg yolks, sugar, and salt in a medium-size glass or metal bowl. Once the water is boiling, reduce the heat to low and fit the bowl snuggly over the pot, whisking the ingredients to prevent curdling. Continue to whisk until the ground cherries soften and the custard has thickened to a texture similar to hollandaise sauce (velvety smooth and coating the back of a spoon dipped into it). This will take about 10 minutes.

Once you have achieved the desired consistency, remove the custard from the heat and whisk in the butter pieces until melted. At this point, I suggest using either a standing blender or handheld immersion blender to blend everything for 1 minute on high for an extra-smooth consistency. Place the custard in a jar, close with a lid, and place in the refrigerator for at least 30 minutes to set and thicken. The custard will last for up to 1 week in the refrigerator.

Make the Cake: Place a rack in the centre of the oven and preheat to 325°F (160°C). Butter three 8-inch (20 cm) round cake pans and flour the insides to coat. Flip the pans to tap out excess flour.

In a large mixing bowl, whisk together the flour blend, baking powder, baking soda, and salt. In a separate large mixing bowl, stir together the carrots, almonds, apricots, and walnuts until combined.

Frosting

8 ounces (226 grams) full-fat cream cheese, room temperature

½ cup (120 grams) unsalted butter, room temperature and cut into 6 pieces

⅛ teaspoon kosher salt

2 cups (240 grams) powdered sugar

In a stand mixer fitted with the paddle attachment, beat the sugar with the oil on medium-high speed until smooth. Add the eggs, one at a time. Continue to beat until the mixture is so smooth it forms ribbons when a spoon runs through it, 5 to 7 minutes. (It may seem like a long time but it's necessary to create an aerated, light crumb.) Reduce the speed to low and gently add the flour mixture ¼ cup at a time, adding more as soon as the flour disappears into the batter. Use a spatula to gently stir in the chunky carrot mixture.

Divide the batter among the prepared pans and bake the cakes until the tops are lightly browned and spring back when gently poked, about 30 minutes. Rotate the pans front to back midway through cooking. Cool the cakes for 10 minutes, then run a knife around the edges of the pans to release the cakes, and carefully invert onto wire racks. Once cooled to room temperature, prepare to frost the cake or, at this point, the layers can be wrapped airtight with plastic wrap and placed in the freezer for up to 2 months; thaw before frosting.

Make the Frosting: While the cakes are baking, in a stand mixer fitted with the paddle attachment, beat the cream cheese and butter together until smooth and creamy. No lumps, please! Add the salt and gradually scoop in the powdered sugar ¼ cup (30 grams) at a time. Continue to beat until the frosting is velvety smooth.

Frost the Cake: Place one layer of cake, top side up, on a serving plate. Spread one-third of the frosting over top. Top with the second cake layer, this time bottom side up. Spoon ⅓ cup of the ground cherry custard over top, leaving a ½-inch (1 cm) border—much like a pizza crust—around the edges (the weight of the last cake layer will push the custard to its edge naturally). Reserve some custard for serving. Top with the final layer of cake, right side up. Use the remaining two-thirds of the frosting to cover the top and sides. Smooth out the frosting and sprinkle (while the frosting is still soft) with chopped walnuts, ground cherries, and sliced almonds.

Place the cake in the refrigerator for 15 minutes to set the frosting. This cake can keep overnight, covered, in the refrigerator. When you are ready to serve, bring the cake to room temperature (this takes about 60 minutes). If you happen to find yourself with extra cake, wrap it once again and store in the refrigerator for up to 4 days.

recipe continues

NOTES

Ground cherries are available at most supermarkets and are abundant at local markets this time of year. If you can't find ground cherries, you can make a lemon custard as a substitute. Substitute ¼ cup ground cherries with ⅓ cup (80 mL) freshly squeezed lemon juice and 1 table-spoon lemon zest.

Egg whites can be reserved and used in a future recipe. Why not have a dessert party and try the Mulberry-Stained Meringue Cookies (page 95)?

I use Bob's Red Mill 1-to-1 Baking Flour, but all-purpose flour works well too.

Dried fruits can soak up moisture from the cake, leaving the cake itself dry. For a moist cake, the apricots need to be soaked. Skipping this step risks a less moist and fluffy cake.

Rhubarb, Bay Leaf & Frangipane Galette

Serves a crowd

The protagonist of this galette is rhubarb—and rhubarb alone, because it's more than a strawberry's sidekick. Its sweet, tangy, deep-red stalks shine in this rustic French tart, and are heightened by the peppery, herbaceous scents of bay leaf. Galettes are a true lesson in the art of imperfection. No two galettes are the same. Many have cracks and crumbles, and no matter the filling, the results turn into something delicious. That is the magic of the galette.

Pastry

1½ cups (190 grams) all-purpose flour

1 tablespoon granulated sugar

½ teaspoon kosher salt

½ cup (120 grams) cold unsalted butter, diced into cubes

¼ cup (60 mL) ice water

Filling

3 to 4 stalks rhubarb

4 fresh bay leaves, minced

¼ (50 grams) cup granulated sugar

Frangipane

½ cup (48 grams) almond flour (or finely ground almonds)

2 tablespoons granulated sugar

¼ teaspoon kosher salt

2 tablespoons (30 grams) unsalted butter, room temperature

1 egg

2 teaspoons pure vanilla extract

To Finish

1 egg, beaten (for the egg wash)

Vanilla ice cream, for serving (optional)

Make the Pastry: In a large bowl, mix the flour, sugar, and salt together. Add the butter cubes and use your fingertips to lightly work the butter into the flour until it's the size of peas (do your best not to let the butter melt in your hands). Add the ice water and continue to use your hands to mix everything together a little more until the dough is crumbly. Lay a large sheet of plastic wrap on a work surface. Place the crumbly pastry dough onto the plastic wrap. Press the dough into a ball and wrap. Set the dough ball aside in the refrigerator until ready to use.

Place a 14-inch (36 cm) square piece of parchment paper onto a clean work surface. Dust the parchment paper with flour and roll out the dough into a 12-inch (30 cm) round. Sprinkle with more flour as needed to prevent it from sticking. Transfer the dough along with the parchment paper to a baking sheet and place in the refrigerator to set for 30 minutes.

Preheat the oven to 400°F (200°C).

Make the Filling: Cut the rhubarb in half lengthwise, then into 1½-inch (4 cm) pieces. In a small bowl, toss the bay leaves with the sugar. Use your fingers to rub the bay leaves with the sugar. This will release some of their aromatics into the sugar. Pour your sugar mixture into a large bowl and add the prepared rhubarb. Mix until the rhubarb is well coated, then set aside.

Make the Frangipane: In a small food processor, combine the almond flour, sugar, salt, butter, egg, and vanilla. Purée until smooth, about 1 minute.

Finish the Galette: Spoon the frangipane into the centre of the rolled-out dough, leaving a 1-inch (2.5 cm) border. Artfully place the rhubarb on top of the frangipane to cover it. I like to angle a row of rhubarb in one direction and then the next row in the opposite direction to form a zigzag of rows. Use the parchment paper as an aid to fold the exposed edge of dough toward the centre, enclosing the filling in a rustic manner. Brush the edge of the dough with your egg wash. Bake for 35 minutes or until the crust is golden and the filling bubbles like a cauldron. Let the galette rest on a cooling rack for 5 to 10 minutes before serving. I love serving it with ice cream, but that is completely optional.

Summer

FROM CORN ON THE COB to juicy peaches, we are now entering Ontario's version of Willy Wonka's factory. Blackberries, mulberries, watermelons, plums, peaches, apricots—it is fruit mania at the markets. What better way to harness the abundance than to make Strawberry Shortcake Scones (page 110) for an easy Sunday brunch? Or to pick a ripened blueberry off the bush as a sweet tender snack?

Summer is an easy time when the sun blankets you and the earth provides this great abundance. Beaches and parks mean less cooking in the kitchen and more prepping on picnic tables. A simple Peach, Burrata & Basil Salad (page 102) needs nothing more than a knife to slice the peach and a few forks for sharing. The ingredients are minimal because peak-summer fruits are like fireworks on their own. It's also time to dust off those grills, because artichokes, eggplants, tomatoes, and zucchinis are popping out of their stalks uncontrollably. Turn your cobs into Curly Corn Ribs with Fresh Zhoug & Shishito Peppers (page 123) and make one or all of these summer favourites: Grilled Artichokes with Whipped Garlic (page 117), Green Tacos with Zucchini Spears (page 129), and Apricot BBQ Sticky Ribs (page 136). The sweetest and stickiest season of the year, summer offers a full-blown list of peak-season treasures.

How To: Make Lavender Almond Milk

Makes 4 cups (1 litre)

My commitment to taking a practical recipe and aggrandizing it knows no boundaries. In this case, with an opulent Ontario flower as my muse, I flipped the classic nut milk on its head and crowned it with the winsome essence of lavender. Adding such an ingredient as lavender to almond milk could be thought of as being extravagant, but I suggest giving it a try. It may even change the way—in the most pleasant sense—that you perceive the flavours. It is refreshing and sweet and something I will drink on its own, sometimes in tea, and most favourably with my Homemade Activated Granola (page 86).

Equipment

1 colander

1 blender

1 cheesecloth, linen cloth, or nut milk bag (see Note)

1 large bowl

Lavender Almond Milk

2 cups raw almonds, soaked overnight

2 teaspoons edible lavender (see Note)

1 tablespoon honey

1 teaspoon pure vanilla extract

Pinch of kosher salt

4½ cups (1.125 litres) filtered water

Step 1: Drain the soaked almonds in a colander and shake well to remove excess liquid.

Step 2: Place the almonds, lavender, honey, vanilla, salt, and water in a blender. Start the blender on a low speed and progress to high. Blend for about 3 minutes, or until everything has fully emulsified.

Step 3: Place a piece of cheesecloth or linen cloth or a nut milk bag over a large bowl and pour the liquid from the blender into the cloth or bag. (If using a cloth, be sure to secure the cloth with string or a large elastic while pouring.) Most of the milk will filter through effortlessly. To extract the remaining milk, gently twist the top of the cloth or bag to encourage the milk to push through. This process will take 5 to 8 minutes. (For an idea of what to do with the remaining almond pulp, see Note.)

Step 4: Pour the lavender almond milk into glasses to serve. The milk can be stored in the refrigerator in sealed containers or jars for up to 5 days.

NOTES

If you do not have cheesecloth or a nut milk bag, use a clean linen cloth. I have a bunch of linen scraps that I use for this, and they work just as well.

There are two main types of lavender that grow in Ontario, and the best for culinary use is English lavender. You can find edible lavender during this time at specialty spice stores, natural food shops, and farmers' markets.

Excess almond pulp can be dried and used as flour in other recipes (see Rhubarb, Bay Leaf & Frangipane Galette, page 78). The best way to dry almond meal is to lay a ¼-inch (0.5 cm) layer across a baking sheet and heat in your oven at its lowest setting. This will differ for every oven, but a general rule of thumb is to heat the pulp for 90 minutes to 2 hours in a 200°F (93°C) oven, stirring every 30 minutes. Give everything a quick blitz in the blender on high speed for 1 to 2 minutes until you have a consistency akin to a grainy flour.

Homemade Activated Granola

Makes 5 cups (1.25 litres)

There is something about the summer that screams "Granola for breakfast!" to me. Maybe it is because there is not much to-do about it, and smoothies have never really been my MO. I like to use a special blend of Ontario's best nuts, seeds, fruits, and provisions for my granola and flood it with one of my favourite June flavours—lavender—particularly my creamy Lavender Almond Milk (page 84). What makes this granola "activated" is that the nuts and seeds are soaked overnight—a little trick I learned as a nutritionist to make everything easier to digest and enhance the value of nutrients they may carry.

1 cup raw almonds, soaked overnight

1 cup raw walnuts, soaked overnight

½ cup sunflower seeds, soaked overnight

½ cup green raisins (see Note)

1 cup chopped dried apples (unsulphured)

½ cup dried mulberries (see Note)

¼ cup buckwheat groats

¼ cup chia seeds

¼ cup hemp hearts

1 tablespoon honey

1 tablespoon extra virgin olive oil

2 teaspoons pure vanilla extract

½ teaspoon kosher salt

Lavender Almond Milk (page 84), for serving

Use a fine-mesh sieve to drain the almonds, walnuts, and sunflower seeds. Rinse the drained nuts and seeds with fresh water and shake the sieve to remove excess liquid.

Preheat the oven to 250°F (120°C) and line a baking sheet with parchment paper.

Roughly chop the almonds and walnuts to get a good mix of large and small pieces. In a large mixing bowl, combine the chopped nuts, sunflower seeds, raisins, dried apples, dried mulberries, buckwheat groats, chia seeds, and hemp hearts and mix well. In a separate bowl, mix together the honey, olive oil, vanilla, and salt. Pour the wet ingredients over the bowl of granola. Use a wooden spoon to mix, thoroughly coating the granola.

Spread the granola evenly onto the prepared baking sheet. Bake until golden, about 25 minutes. (To brown the granola evenly, remove the baking sheet from the oven every 10 minutes and give it a good shake.) Cool the granola for 15 minutes. This will help crisp up the granola but not fully toast it. Serve warm with lavender almond milk or store in an airtight container for up to 1 week.

NOTES

Green raisins are less overpowering than dark raisins. If you have trouble finding these at a bulk store, add ½ cup chopped dried apricots instead.

Dried mulberries can be found at most bulk stores, but if you have trouble finding them, use an extra ½ cup chopped dried apples.

Arctic Char with Garlic Scape Pesto
Serves 4

Of all the fast suppers, fish is what I turn to most. Begin with a mild fish like Arctic char—much less fishy than salmon despite looking similar—and pair with a pungent sauce. This pesto is made mostly of garlic scapes—a spirally green stalk divorced from its own (garlic) bulb. Scapes are innately garlicky in flavour, so there is not much else to add. I like to whiz in a few leafy greens, some walnuts, and a delicate oil. With few ingredients, some more eccentric than others, this pesto is a bit different, yet familiar—a quality I like to have in my cooking.

Garlic Scape Pesto

8 large garlic scapes, woody bulbs removed and the remainder cut into ½-inch (1 cm) pieces

1 cup sorrel (or arugula)

½ teaspoon kosher salt, plus more to season

¾ cup (180 mL) walnut oil (see Note)

¼ cup (60 mL) white wine vinegar

½ cup raw walnuts

Arctic Char

1 Arctic char fillet (1 pound/ 450 grams)

Kosher salt and freshly cracked black pepper

A few sprigs fresh thyme

A few sprigs fresh rosemary

4 garlic scapes, fully intact

1 handful raw walnuts, for garnish (optional)

Good-quality extra virgin olive oil, for drizzling

Make the Garlic Scape Pesto: Set a large pot of water with a steam insert over high heat. Let the water boil, then add the garlic scapes to the steamer and blanch for 2 minutes. Remove and rinse in cool water (see Note). Place the blanched scapes in a food processor and add the sorrel and salt. Process while slowly adding the walnut oil and then the vinegar. If the pesto begins to gather at the edges, turn off the processor and use a rubber spatula to scrape down the sides, then continue processing. Once a chunky paste has formed, add the walnuts. Pulse the processor until the nuts are completely chopped and a coarse paste has formed. A little texture is a good thing here.

Prepare the Arctic Char: Season the Arctic char with salt and pepper. Set in the refrigerator for a minimum of 20 minutes. Preheat the oven to 425°F (220°C) and line a baking sheet with parchment paper.

Place the seasoned char on the prepared sheet. Scatter the thyme and rosemary sprigs, garlic scapes, and walnuts around the fish. Drizzle lightly with oil. Roast until the fish has cooked through and reaches an internal temperature of 145°F (63°C) on an instant-read thermometer, about 20 minutes.

Plate the fish with the herbs and scapes directly from the baking sheet, and garnish with walnuts. Set aside to cool for 5 minutes before serving with the pesto.

NOTES

Grown in Canada, walnuts add a beautiful delicate flavour to this dish. Walnut oil is an uncommon pantry ingredient and can be expensive. If you do not have walnut oil on hand, a good olive oil for dressing is your second-best friend.

I recommend blanching the scapes prior to processing, to cut the sharpness of the raw garlic taste while keeping the flavour intact.

Basil Ginger Halibut en Papillote

Serves 4

En papillote is a method of cooking and serving fish or other ingredients in a parcel, with minimal clean up after the meal. A short preparation of mincing and chopping, a few folds of paper, 15 minutes in the oven, and you are ready to eat with few dirty dishes to perturb you. The ingredients here are meant to be a guideline to your own adventure. I love greens, so I have included a generous serving here. I like a 1:1 ratio of greens to fish, but this is now your meal, so do as you please.

4 halibut fillets (each 4 ounces/ 110 grams)

Kosher salt, for seasoning

2 tablespoons minced fresh ginger

4 cloves garlic, minced

1 cup basil leaves

4 cups baby bok choy, quartered (see Note)

4 teaspoons extra virgin olive oil

1 pound (450 grams) soba noodles

¼ cup quick pickled onions (page 184)

¼ cup (60 mL) rice vinegar

Flaky sea salt, to season

NOTE: *Please adjust the ratio of bok choy to fish to suit your tastes. If you don't have bok choy, there are a lot of options for substitution, like ribboned chard or bunched spinach, so use what you have or what is in season.*

Measure out four 14-inch (36 cm) square pieces of parchment paper, and preheat the oven to 350°F (175°C).

Place a halibut fillet in the centre of each piece of parchment and season each with kosher salt. Layer equal amounts of the ginger, garlic, basil, and bok choy over the pieces of fish. Fold each parchment paper over the fish, folding the edges several times to form a sealed envelope. Place the envelopes onto a baking sheet and brush the tops of each packet with 1 teaspoon olive oil. Bake in the oven until the bok choy is tender and the fish is flaky and no longer translucent in the centre, 15 to 20 minutes. Remove from the oven and set aside for serving.

Bring a large pot of water to a boil. Gently lower the soba noodles into the boiling water to avoid hot cannonball splashes. Cook for 2 to 3 minutes, until soft. Drain the noodles into a colander and rinse with cold water. Shake the colander to drain any excess water. Set aside for serving.

In four wide plates or shallow bowls, arrange a bed of soba noodles. Lay the halibut over the noodles and invite the baby bok choy to rest with the fish. Top each plate with 1 tablespoon pickled onions, any extra basil leaves you have sitting around, and a quick splash of rice vinegar. Give the dish a little taste and season with sea salt, if needed, before serving.

Cardamom Rose Visiting Cake

Makes one 5- × 9-inch (12 × 23 cm) loaf

This cake tastes as beautiful as it looks. There is a gentleness and precision involved when it comes to baking with flowers. The fruity and slightly earthy taste of the cardamom complements and harnesses the distinctly strong "pretty" flavour of an early summer rose. (Some may say these two act as soulmates to the tongue.) This is the type of cake I bake in batches, freeze (unglazed), and have on hand for special occasions.

Cake

1 cup (200 grams) granulated sugar, plus more for sprinkling

1½ teaspoons ground cardamom

2 eggs, room temperature

¼ teaspoon kosher salt

2 tablespoons rosewater

1 cup (125 grams) all-purpose flour, plus more for coating the pan

8 tablespoons (120 grams) unsalted butter, melted and cooled, plus more for greasing the pan

Icing *(optional)*

½ tablespoon unsalted butter, melted

½ cup (60 grams) powdered sugar

½ tablespoon whole milk

For Topping

¼ cup sliced almonds

Edible flowers or rose petals, for garnish

Make the Cake: Preheat the oven to 350°F (175°C). Lightly grease a 5- × 9-inch (12 × 23 cm) loaf pan with butter, then coat with flour.

In a medium bowl, use your fingers to mix the sugar with the ground cardamom until well combined. Whisk in the eggs one at a time until everything is blended into a custard-like dough. Whisk in the salt and rosewater. Switch to a rubber spatula and stir in the flour. Finally, fold in the melted butter.

Scrape the batter into the prepared loaf pan and smooth the top with the spatula. Place your loaf pan on a baking sheet and bake until golden and a little crisp on the outside, 25 to 30 minutes. The inside will remain moist. Let the cake cool for 5 minutes, then run a thin knife around the sides to loosen it. Lay a flat plate over the top of the loaf pan. Carefully flip the cake over and give the bottom of the pan a tap. Lift the pan off the plate and use a second plate to repeat this method, turning your cake back to its upright position.

Make the Icing (Optional): While the cake is baking, in a medium bowl, whisk the melted butter with the powdered sugar. Add the milk and continue to whisk until there are no lumps. Once the cake is cool to the touch, use a pastry brush to ice the top of the cake. The amount of icing is a personal decision, but remember that the icing will thicken as it sits and hardens.

If you have iced your cake, scatter the sliced almonds and edible flowers over the top before the icing sets and hardens. Otherwise, you can serve the cake warm or cool. If serving cool without icing, a sprinkling of a little extra sugar goes a long way. When well wrapped in plastic wrap or sealed in an airtight container, this cake will keep for about 5 days at room temperature or up to 2 months in the freezer.

Mulberry-Stained Meringue Cookies

Makes 6 to 8 cookies

These meringue cookies are crisp white wafers with a marshmallow inside. I like to keep the meringue dollops messy and on the large side. It brings character and allows for a beautiful presentation when the billowing folds are cracked enough to let a few mulberries stain their gooey centres. The mulberries I find in Ontario are black; they are native to Canada and are available only in June and July. They look similar to blackberries but are a little sweeter and chewier—the alto to blackberries' baritone. Mulberries are by far my favourite fruit and I would love for you to try them, but if you can't pick your own—sadly, they are not sold in grocery stores and rarely at the farmers' market because they squish all too easily—you can use any sort of berry here instead.

---

4 egg whites, room temperature (see Note)

⅛ teaspoon cream of tartar

⅛ teaspoon kosher salt

1 cup (200 grams) granulated sugar

1 teaspoon pure vanilla extract

2 cups mulberries (or raspberries or blackberries)

NOTES

Egg yolks can be reserved and used in a future recipe. Why not have a dessert party and try the Chickadee Carrot Cake with Ground Cherry Custard (page 74)?

The biggest enemy of egg whites fluffing is fat. Make sure there is no morsel of yolk or butter in the bowl before whisking,

Preheat the oven to 225°F (110°C) and line a baking sheet with parchment paper.

Place the egg whites, cream of tartar, and salt in a medium mixing bowl or a stand mixer fitted with the whisk attachment (clean and free from any moisture, see Note). Turn on the mixer (or use a handheld electric mixer) and mix on low speed until the egg whites foam. Increase the speed to high and gradually add the sugar, one large spoonful at a time. Add more sugar as soon as the last spoonful has dissolved. (To test this, rub a small bit of the mixture between your fingers. If it feels gritty, the sugar has not fully dissolved.) Continue to beat until stiff peaks form, then gently stir in the vanilla. Use a large spoon to scoop out about ¼ cup (60 mL) of the fluffy meringue onto the prepared baking sheet. Do not sweat over distancing the meringues; they will not spread like cookies when they bake. Repeat with the rest of the meringue.

Bake for 1 hour. Turn off the oven after the allotted time and place a wooden spoon in the door to let the oven cool with the baking sheet full of meringues still in the oven. This will allow the meringues to cool completely and crisp up nicely. Even better, let them sleep over in the oven (they like the dry heat and will be ready for you the next day). No babysitting required. If you choose to store them in an airtight container, place them in the refrigerator and avoid high-moisture areas, as this can soften your meringues.

The meringues are best when cracked with a spoon and showered with mulberries that bleed into every sweet crevice.

How To: Make a Garlic Pizza Bianca

Makes one 12-inch (30 cm) pizza

Note: This recipe needs to be prepared 24 hours in advance, and you will need a kitchen scale.

Recreating a pizza without a wood-fire oven is much easier when you cast away the dream of owning such an oven and work with what you've got. A smooth-running kitchen oven will do a fine job. At this point, all you need is a good recipe that caters to what you have. There are many ways to make a pizza, but this is the one I am loyal to. The crust comes out Neapolitan-style—a thin, pillowy chew with a slightly thicker and crisp edge. A commendable vessel for a simple pizza like Pizza Bianca—a "white pizza." In this pizza, the tomato takes a step back to let olive oil have centre stage. The toppings are minimal, but it's a good opportunity to focus on using peak-season ingredients, such as a single heirloom tomato—freckled shoulders are quite all right as long as the fruity, grassy flavours stay sharp on the tongue, like those of a good field tomato will do. And for total harmony, add a copious haze of olive oil and garlic to the fresh dough. Combined, these ingredients will make you weep. To freshen things up, I like a little sweet fennel seed too. Finally, for a mix of texture and tradition, creamy mozzarella and Parmesan bubble and melt into every dimple this dough has. That's it. No sauce, no fuss.

Equipment

1 kitchen scale

1 large mixing bowl

1 clean tea towel

1 container or bowl (8 quarts/8 litres)

1 pizza sheet or stone
    (12 inches/30 cm in diameter)

Pizza Dough *(everything must be measured by weight to get this one right)*

173 grams lukewarm water

3 grams granulated sugar

2 grams instant dry yeast

10 grams extra virgin olive oil

230 grams "00" flour

6 grams kosher salt

Step 1: To make the pizza dough, mix the water, sugar, and yeast together in a large bowl. Let sit for 10 minutes. Once the mixture begins to bubble, you know that the yeast is active and ready. Whisk in the oil. Once everything is well combined, give it another whisk and add the flour to the liquid. Use your hands to mix in the flour and knead the dough in the bowl until the flour is fully mixed in. Don't worry if the mixture is a little lumpy. Cover with a tea towel and set aside for 20 to 30 minutes.

Step 2: Once the dough has had a rest, uncover and add the salt. Continue to knead until all of the salt is incorporated. Cover the dough again and let sit on the counter at room temperature for an hour to begin its rise. For the next rise, the dough needs a large container in order to rise at least double in size. Transfer the dough to a larger bowl if necessary. Cover the bowl with plastic wrap and refrigerate overnight for a cold rise.

recipe continues

Toppings

3 tablespoons extra virgin olive oil

2 cloves garlic, minced

1 tablespoon fennel seeds

2 tablespoons dried oregano

1 heirloom tomato, sliced

4½ ounces (125 grams) fresh mozzarella, torn

¼ cup (0.9 ounce/25 grams) freshly grated Parmesan

1 bunch fresh basil leaves, for topping

Step 3: Two hours before you intend to eat, lightly oil a pizza sheet and transfer the dough onto the sheet. With oiled hands, press the dough down as best as you can (the dough may be a bit tough and not fill the sheet yet). Cover the dough on the sheet with a tea towel and set it on the counter at room temperature for 30 minutes.

Step 4: After the elapsed time, press down the dough again. Repeat in 30-minute intervals until the dough fits the sheet with an equal amount of thickness all around. It usually takes me two to three times.

Step 5: Place one wire rack at the lowest level and one wire rack in the centre of the oven. Preheat the oven to 500°F (260°C). Par-bake the dough with no toppings on the lowest rack for 6 to 8 minutes, until the dough has set and the bottom is golden brown. Remove from the oven. Turn the oven temperature down to 475°F (250°C).

Step 6: Add the toppings. Evenly spread the oil, garlic, fennel seeds, and oregano on the par-baked pizza. Top with the tomato slices and mozzarella. Sprinkle the Parmesan over the pizza, covering all the way to the edge to get that fried cheese crust everyone loves. Place the pizza in the centre rack of the oven and bake until the cheese on the edge is set and the crust achieves the desired leoparding (mini bubbles with black spots), 15 to 20 minutes (see Note). Use a flat spatula to help get the pizza and excess cheese off the sheet. Top with fresh basil, slice, and serve.

NOTES

Making your own dough requires preparation the night before serving the pizza. If you don't have time, skip this step but find a good bakery where you can source quality dough.

Every oven is different. Keep a close eye near the end of the bake. I don't want you to lose all your efforts to a bad burn.

Seared Cod with Summer Fennel & Pea Ceviche & Pickled Rhubarb

Serves 4

Cod, to me, is the queen of all fish. If you can get your hands on a good BC-caught or Marine Stewardship Council–certified fillet, take good care of her and she will return the favour with her velvety texture. Snap peas are in peak season at this time, and you will notice that in July, even on their own, they are naturally sweet like candy. By soaking them in lemon juice along with fennel, mimicking a ceviche, a complex balance of sweet and tangy flavours develops that brings a certain vibrancy to the dish. As does the pickled rhubarb, another seasonal gift that brightens the colours of the plate and adds a distinct sharpness to the palate. The assembly of such strong flavours works beautifully with a mild buttery fish like cod. Something cooling to enjoy on a hot summer day.

Quick Pickled Rhubarb

2 stalks rhubarb (with a thickness similar to a candlestick), sliced into 3-inch (8 cm) long batons (see Note)

½ cup (125 mL) red wine vinegar

1½ teaspoons kosher salt, plus more to season

¾ cup (180 mL) water

¼ cup (60 mL) honey

Summer Fennel & Pea Ceviche

2 cups fresh snap peas, finely julienned

½ fennel (10 ounces/275 grams), shaved paper-thin (see Note)

Zest and juice of 1 lemon

1 clove garlic, minced

Make the Quick Pickled Rhubarb: Pack a sterilized 3-cup (750 mL) sealable jar with the rhubarb batons until the jar is three-quarters full.

In a small saucepan, bring the vinegar, salt, and water to a boil. Reduce the heat to medium and stir in the honey. Continue to stir until the honey and salt have fully dissolved. Pour the hot liquid into the jar, enough to cover the rhubarb batons plus ½ inch (1 cm). Set aside until the liquid cools to room temperature. Seal the jar with its lid and chill in the refrigerator until cold, at least 1 hour. Quick pickled rhubarb can last for up to 1 week in the refrigerator.

Make the Summer Fennel & Pea Ceviche: In a medium mixing bowl, combine the peas, fennel, lemon zest, lemon juice, and garlic until the vegetables are well coated. Set aside for a minimum of 5 minutes.

recipe continues

4 black cod fillets (each 4 ounces/
   110 grams), skin on

Fine sea salt and freshly cracked
   black pepper

1 tablespoon extra virgin olive oil

½ cup (125 mL) Quick Pickled
   Rhubarb

½ teaspoon dried chili flakes

Good-quality extra virgin olive oil,
   for drizzling

Prepare the Cod: Season the cod fillets with salt and pepper. In a large skillet over medium-high, heat the oil. Place the cod, skin side down, in the skillet. Cook until the skin has browned and crisped, 5 to 6 minutes (if you try to flip before the skin has crisped, the skin will stick to the skillet and result in one big fish mess. The fish will loosen when it is ready to be flipped). Turn the fish and cook until flaky and nearly opaque in the centre, 2 to 4 minutes more.

When ready to serve, thinly slice the pickled rhubarb cross-wise into ⅛ inch thick rounds. Plate the fennel and pea ceviche. Top the ceviche with the crispy skinned cod and pickled rhubarb batons. Season with chili flakes, salt, and pepper. Drizzle with olive oil and serve.

NOTES

Two basic types of rhubarb are found in Ontario markets: the older, traditional variety with thicker, greener stalks and the deep pink, slender-stalked variety. The latter certainly makes for brighter dishes and the concentrated colour can sometimes indicate a tarter stalk. For this recipe, what you choose is entirely up to you—either variety will work. Once rhubarb is pickled to perfection, you will be adding it to many more dishes.

When cutting vegetables paper-thin, I like to use a staple in my kitchen: the vegetable peeler. A mandoline works just as well here too.

Peach, Burrata & Basil Salad

Serves 6

Peaches are a quintessential summer fruit, and as you'll see in this dish, this is the time of year to remind yourself that simple food is best. The secret to a good peach salad is to use fruit at its peak ripeness—as is the case in July in Ontario. A ripe peach gives a little when squeezed, and when the sun is high in the sky, a peach will set off a sweet fragrance. That is how you know your peach is ready. But who needs all of those details when the best test is to taste it? Bite into one and let the juice spill down your chin, onto your fingers, and down your forearm.

Here we lay a bed of peach slices across a plate as if they were a picnic blanket bracing the very large misshapen ball of burrata that is to be cut down the centre, only to let cream ooze out onto each slice. Finish with a scoop of vinegary pink pickled onions and brighten the dish with a bit of fresh basil to clean the palate. I like freestone peaches (easy to remove from the pit) for slicing and clingstone for handheld eating, but when given no choice, the ripest of any variety will taste best. This salad is spectacular on its own, but it goes well with a nice barbecue dinner like Prince Apple Elk Burgers (page 73).

10 peaches, stoned and sliced

20 fresh basil leaves

1 ball burrata (8.8 ounces/ 250 grams)

3 tablespoons quick pickled onions, including the brine (page 184)

Flaky sea salt or finishing salt and freshly cracked black pepper

3 tablespoons good-quality extra virgin olive oil

Decorate a serving plate with the peach slices and basil leaves. Top with the burrata and pickled onions, along with a spoonful or two of the pickling brine. Season with salt and pepper, then drizzle with olive oil and serve.

Kohlrabi, Fennel, Cherry & Toasted Walnut Salad

Serves 4

This is the type of unfussy salad that serves both purpose and pleasure. The foundation is a bulb-like vegetable called kohlrabi. The flavour of kohlrabi is much like a sweeter broccoli stem and the texture is crisp like an apple. Slice your kohlrabi paper-thin, just as you do with the fennel, and add as many cherries as you possibly can. Cherries are in season from June to August but at their sweetest in July— rich in flavour, and unspeakably juicy. And if you are thinking of skipping the toasted walnut step, think again—the walnuts add wonderful nutty richness to the salad.

Lemon Honey Dressing

⅓ cup (80 mL) good-quality extra virgin olive oil

2 tablespoons honey

Juice of ½ lemon

Kosher salt, to season

Salad

½ cup raw walnut halves

2 kohlrabi (see Note)

½ fennel (with fronds)

¾ cup pitted and halved cherries

NOTE: *Both the stems and leaves of kohlrabi can be used, but for this recipe, we can reserve the stems for another day (try them in my Roasted Ruby Radish on Herbed Torn Greens, page 66).*

In a small mixing bowl, whisk together the oil, honey, lemon juice, and salt. Set aside for serving.

Heat a medium skillet over medium-high. Once the surface of the skillet is hot, add the walnuts to toast. Shake the skillet occasionally to ensure all sides of the nuts are well toasted and no nut comes out burnt. This will take no more than 5 minutes. Remove from the heat and let cool. Once cool, roughly chop the walnuts into pieces and set aside.

To peel the kohlrabi, begin by removing excess leaves attached to the bulb. Cut both the top and butt of the kohlrabi so the extra knobs don't get in the way and it can sit flat on the cutting board. Use a vegetable peeler or sharp paring knife to peel the sides, rotating the bulb as you go. With a mandoline or a large vegetable peeler, thinly slice the kohlrabi into paper-thin rounds.

Use a chef's knife to remove the woody bottom end of the fennel and cut off the stalks with fronds. Set aside the stalks. Using a chef's knife, vegetable peeler, or mandoline, slice the fennel into slices as paper-thin as the kohlrabi. Pluck a few of the fronds off the stalks to use as garnish.

Plate the salad on a large serving platter. Begin with a layer of kohlrabi rounds, followed by fennel slices and cherries. Pour the dressing over the salad and toss to coat before garnishing with walnuts and fennel fronds.

Jamaican Beef Patties with Jalapeño Peach Sauce

Serves 4

In the summer, there's a notion that we are to divorce the kitchen oven and leave it to hibernate until the return of winter, but every once in a while, a good recipe comes along—like this one—that convinces me otherwise. In this case, I would like you to consider Jamaican Beef Patties, a Caribbean version of the Cornish pasty brought to the region by British colonists. The neon-yellow, flaky handheld meal is delicious and makes for the ultimate street food. I am by no means a master of Jamaican cuisine, but I am a master at eating these. Toronto has a large Jamaican population and thanks to that very alive and present Caribbean cuisine, Jamaican patties have become an essential snack in this city. And if you by chance find yourself in Leslieville, my farmer friend, Annette Jennings, makes pretty extraordinary Jamaican food at my local farmers' market.

My flaky pie crust comes with a multitude of flavours, including turmeric to keep that classic canary-yellow crust. (I also recommend making larger batches of these patties and freezing them for a later time; they make for a very filling post-work or after-school snack.) While you could make these patties year-round, I've included this recipe here because I love eating them dipped in my Jalapeño Peach Sauce, something not-so-traditional for the handheld patty, often eaten without any sauce at all. Both the jalapeño and peach are at their peak and the sweet and spicy sauce complements the jerk-spiced beef really well.

Patty Dough

2 cups (250 grams) all-purpose flour, plus more for dusting

2 tablespoons baking powder

2 teaspoons ground turmeric

¼ teaspoon kosher salt

½ cup (120 grams) cold unsalted butter

½ cup (125 mL) ice water

Beef Filling

4 ounces (110 grams) lean ground beef

¼ teaspoon kosher salt

2 tablespoons jerk spice

3 tablespoons extra virgin olive oil, divided

1 yellow onion, peeled and finely diced

2 cloves garlic, minced

Make the Patty Dough: In a large bowl, mix the flour, baking powder, turmeric, and salt to combine. Using your hands, rub the butter into the flour until the flour looks crumbly. Move quickly, as the heat of your hands will melt the butter otherwise. Pour in the ice water and use your hands to mix, forming the dough into one large ball. Cut the dough into four equal pieces, wrap in plastic wrap, and set aside in the refrigerator for 1 hour.

Make the Beef Filling: In a large mixing bowl, combine the beef with the salt and jerk spice. Set aside. In a large skillet over medium, heat 1 tablespoon olive oil. Add the onions and sauté, stirring frequently, until they become translucent, 6 to 8 minutes. Add the garlic and continue to sauté for another 2 minutes. Add the jerk-spiced beef and continue to stir until the beef is fully browned and cooked through, 8 to 10 minutes. Remove the filling from the skillet and set aside to cool (spread the filling across a large plate or baking sheet to help it cool quicker—this will take about 15 minutes).

recipe continues

Jalapeño Peach Sauce

½ jalapeño pepper, seeds removed

2 peaches, stoned

1 tablespoon honey

¾ cup fresh cilantro leaves

¾ cup ground cherries (see Note)

1 clove garlic

½ cup (125 mL) extra virgin olive oil

Juice of 1 lime

Kosher salt, to season

Preheat the oven to 350°F (175°C) and line a baking sheet with parchment paper.

Make and Bake the Patties: On a lightly floured work surface, roll out the four dough pieces into four circles ½ inch (1 cm) thick (circles will be about the size of a side plate). Place 3 tablespoons of the beef mixture into the centre of each circle. With wet fingers, trace the edges of the dough circle. Fold the dough circles in half and press the edges to seal. Use a fork to crimp the edges and ensure the patty is now sealed well. (This will stop any possible leaks while cooking.) Sometimes my folds have a lot of extra dough around the edges where there isn't filling. If you're experiencing this too, use a paring knife to cut off the excess pastry. Use a pastry brush to coat the tops and edges of each patty with the remaining olive oil, ½ tablespoon each. Place the patties on the prepared baking sheet and bake until lightly browned, 30 minutes. Remove the patties from the oven and set aside to cool for 5 minutes before serving.

Make the Jalapeño Peach Sauce: While the patties are baking, in the bowl of a food processor, place the jalapeño, peaches, honey, cilantro, ground cherries, and garlic and process for 2 minutes or until a coarse well-blended mixture forms. Slowly begin to add the oil and continue processing for 1 to 2 minutes more. If the ingredients stick to the edges of the processor, stop and use a spatula to scrape down the sides. Add the lime juice and process for another minute, until all ingredients are well processed into a thick sauce. Transfer the sauce to a small serving bowl and season with salt. This sauce can be stored in a sealed container in the refrigerator for up to 5 days.

Serve the cooled but still-warm patties with the jalapeño peach sauce.

NOTE: *Ground cherries are available at most supermarkets and are abundant at local markets this time of year. If you can't find ground cherries, you can use the juice of two additional limes as a substitute.*

Grilled Okra & Variety Beans

Serves 6

Most people hear the word okra *and they think Louisiana gumbo, but okra plays a big role in South Asian, Ethiopian, and South African cuisines too. You can find it and variety beans—an assortment of string beans ranging in colour that are at their peak in July—at farmers' markets and grocery stores that specialize in local produce. I find grilling variety beans and okra brings out their natural sweetness—the exterior caramelizes and crisps up while the interior softens, giving both earthy greens (or sometimes purples) a mouthwatering crunch. Their flavours are so delightful, they need only minor embellishment—a zest of a lemon is all—and they are ready to be eaten alongside whatever meal you so choose—but might I suggest the Jamaican Beef Patties (page 107).*

2 cups (200 grams) okra, stems removed

2 cups (270 grams) variety beans (green and purple string beans), trimmed

3 tablespoons extra virgin olive oil

Zest and juice of 1 lemon

Flaky sea salt and freshly cracked black pepper

NOTE: *If you don't have access to a grill, you can use an oven instead. Preheat to 400°F (200°C) and cook the beans and okra on a parchment-lined baking sheet for 12 to 16 minutes, turning once midway.*

Preheat the grill to medium-high heat.

In a large mixing bowl, coat the okra and beans with the oil and lemon juice. Place the okra and beans on a grill pan and cook on the grill until charred, about 2 minutes per side (see Note). Transfer the okra and beans to the mixing bowl. Season with the lemon zest, salt, and pepper before serving.

Strawberry Shortcake Scones

Makes 10 to 12 scones

Scones are best served warm, split in half so their steam can cascade out in its hot golden glory. Their air pockets are a warm welcome to be lavished with a dollop of cream and the best flavours the summer has to offer—like a vibrant and aromatic July strawberry, perfectly ripened by time and sun.

2 cups (250 grams) all-purpose flour

2 tablespoons granulated sugar

1 tablespoon baking powder

1 teaspoon baking soda

1½ teaspoons kosher salt

½ cup (120 grams) cold unsalted butter, cut into 1-inch (2.5 cm) cubes

¾ cup (175 mL) buttermilk

2 cups strawberries, hulled and halved

1 cup (250 mL) heavy cream, whipped

NOTE: *Strawberries tend to have a Goldilocks complex, as they need the days to be just hot enough to ripen and the nights cool enough to rest and replenish. July is the perfect time to make this recipe.*

Sift the flour into a large mixing bowl. Mix in the sugar, baking powder, baking soda, and salt. Work the butter in by hand until the flour mixture forms a coarse meal. Make a well in the centre of the flour. Using a fork, gently stir the buttermilk in just until the dough, which will be wet and sticky, comes together—no more, no less. (Unlike bread dough, where kneading is needed to align the gluten structure, scones turn rock hard if that gluten structure forms. For a tender and flaky scone, do not overwork the dough.) Stop once everything is cohesive. Gently knead the dough, still in the bowl, with a light touch of your hands as if you were shaping the most beautiful ceramic vase on a pottery wheel, 8 to 10 times. Cover the dough with a clean tea towel and chill in the refrigerator for 30 minutes.

Preheat the oven to 375°F (190°C) and line a baking sheet with parchment paper.

On a lightly floured work surface, roll out the dough to ¾ inch (2 cm) thick. Cut the dough with the rim of a tumbler or a sharp scone cutter (somewhere near the 2½-inch/6 cm diameter mark) that has been lightly floured. Repeat until you have made as many dough rounds as possible.

Place the dough rounds on the prepared baking sheet. Bake until the scones are golden, about 20 minutes. Set aside to cool for 8 minutes before serving. These scones are best served to your guests warm, ready to be torn in half with lots of sweet strawberries and billowy whipped cream.

Do your best to serve as soon as they are made. Any leftovers—if there are any—can be wrapped airtight as soon as they cool to room temperature and frozen for up to 2 months. Frozen scones can be reheated in a 350°F (175°C) oven for 5 to 10 minutes.

Creamy Strawberry Rhubarb Porridge
Serves 4

No matter the weather, the scent of stewing fruits and warm oats is always a ready welcome on my break-fast table. It is the sweet aromas of strawberries and rhubarb at their peak (in July) that does it for me. If not a tart, what better way to enjoy this combination than with a creamy bowl of oats? Take the time to slow-cook your steel-cut oats the night before serving. There are few things as luxurious as a perfectly cooked oats, and this small detail will promise a smooth and decadent breakfast.

Porridge
½ tablespoon extra virgin olive oil

1 cup (140 grams) steel-cut oats

3 cups (750 mL) water

Kosher salt, to season

½ cup (125 mL) oat milk (or any milk)

Strawberry Rhubarb Compote
½ cup strawberries, hulled and halved

¼ cup diced rhubarb

1 tablespoon honey

2 tablespoons water

Plain yogurt, for serving (optional)

Start the porridge the evening before you want to eat it. In a 2-quart (2-litre) saucepan over medium, heat the oil. Add the oats and fry until fragrant, 2 to 3 minutes. Add the water and give the oats a good seasoning of salt. Increase the heat to high and stir every so often until the oats reach a boil. Take the oats off the heat and cover to sit on the stove overnight.

The following morning, uncover the saucepan and stir in the oat milk. Heat the saucepan over medium to bring the porridge back up to a simmer.

While the oats simmer, heat a small saucepan over medium-high. Add the strawberries, rhubarb, honey, and water. Continue to stir to avoid burning the ingredients. Once bubbles begin to form, reduce the heat to a low simmer. Cook until the fruit is soft and the liquid has completely reduced, 10 to 12 minutes, stirring every so often.

Once the porridge has reached a desired serving temperature, remove from the heat to serve with strawberry rhubarb compote and a dollop of yogurt. If you haven't already licked the strawberry rhubarb bowl clean, extras can be stored in a sealed jar or airtight container in the refrigerator for up to 1 week. Porridge can also be stored in a sealed container in the refrigerator for up to 2 days.

How To: Make Farmer's Cheese & Fresh Ricotta

Makes 1½ cups (375 mL) farmer's cheese or 2 cups (500 mL) ricotta

Cheese has always been a food that is both sophisticated and simple. If you have ever made a meal out of an array of cheese and maybe some fresh bread, whispered to yourself, "Bon appétit," and dug in, you know exactly what I mean. Like wine, each kind of cheese has an unmistakable taste (grassy, nutty, floral, earthy, sweet). Farmer's cheese and fresh ricotta are subtle in flavour; when made fresh they are rich and creamy, and they are wonderful blank canvases on which to layer your favourite seasonal treasures. When I taught in the kitchen at Evergreen Brick Works during market days, this recipe was always a major success. It is the easiest way to make cheese and something to feel accomplished about. Anyone who has made their own cheese will say the freshness of its flavour is undeniable compared to store-bought. In this recipe, you can go the farmer's cheese route, which is a firmer, crumblier cheese, or opt for the ricotta, a creamier, milder cousin. No matter the cheese, if it satisfies you, that is all the nourishment you need.

Equipment

1 heavy pot (4 quarts/4 litres)

1 colander

1 large mixing bowl (at least 5 inches/12 cm deep)

1 clean tea towel or cheesecloth

1 slotted spoon

Kitchen twine

1 long kitchen spoon

Fresh Ricotta & Farmer's Cheese

8 cups (2 litres) whole milk

½ cup (125 mL) white wine vinegar

1 teaspoon kosher salt

Step 1: Pour the whole milk into the pot and bring to a slow boil over medium-low. Once the milk begins to steam but has not quite reached a boil (190°F/88°C on a cooking thermometer), remove the milk from the heat. Stir in the vinegar and set the milk mixture aside to rest for 15 minutes while the curds begin to form.

Step 2: Set a colander over a large mixing bowl and line the colander with a damp tea towel or cheesecloth. Use a slotted spoon to transfer the big curds from the pot into the colander. Pour the remaining curds and the excess liquid (the whey) through the cloth.

For Fresh Ricotta

Step 3: Season the cheese curds with salt and let drain anywhere between 10 to 40 minutes. This will depend on how you would like to use your ricotta. Ten minutes will result in a wetter, looser ricotta, best used on pizza or pasta. Forty minutes will result in a drier, firm ricotta, best used for desserts or slathered on toast. Once the ricotta has drained, store in an airtight container for up to 1 week. The whey can be reserved and used as a water substitute when baking breads and pizzas—it will give an extra tang to your dough—or can be added to smoothies.

recipe continues

For Farmer's Cheese

Step 3: Season the cheese curds with salt. Wrap and twist the cloth around the cheese curds to squeeze out any remaining juices and form a ball. Use a bit of kitchen twine to attach the ball to a long kitchen spoon or spatula handle, then place the spoon or spatula across the bowl to suspend the ball over the bowl. Gravity will help shape the cheese into a ball. Place in the refrigerator to set for a minimum of 1 hour or overnight.

The main difference between farmer's cheese and ricotta is flavour. Since the farmer's cheese sets for a minimum of 1 hour, it will be much firmer and crumblier than a young ricotta, so serve your farmer's cheese the way you would if you had an extra-flavourful firm ricotta. Store any extras of either cheese in an airtight container in the refrigerator for up to 1 week.

Grilled Artichokes with Whipped Garlic

Serves 4

The globe artichoke is a beautiful cactus-like vegetable that originates in the Mediterranean and knows how to thrive in temperate climates like the Great Lakes region. They are most alluring in August when their scaled petals are still tightly packed and have yet to bloom—this is when the heart is most tender and creamy like an avocado. I like to grill them for 1 to 2 minutes just to add that summer smokiness to the dish. Their fuzzy insides make them a little finicky to prepare, but the value of the meal is measured not by volume but rather by taste and experience. This dish makes for an exciting starter to share among friends on a warm summer evening. Each leaf can be dipped in whipped garlic before teething out the ivory fleshy bits, and when you have reached the end of all your artichoke petals, all is revealed: the meaty artichoke heart in all of its nutty, creamy entirety.

Whipped Garlic

1 cup cloves garlic (see Note)

1 teaspoon kosher salt

4 cups (1 litre) canola oil, divided
(see Note)

¼ cup (60 mL) freshly squeezed
lemon juice

4 artichokes

2 tablespoons extra virgin olive oil

Kosher salt and freshly cracked
black pepper

Make the Whipped Garlic: In the small bowl of a large food processor, process the garlic cloves and salt until the garlic has puréed. If the garlic sticks to the side, stop the processor and use a spatula to scrape the garlic back into the centre of the bowl. Once the garlic purée is smooth, transfer the purée to the larger processing bowl and continue processing on low speed as you slowly drizzle 1 tablespoon canola oil through the tube. Process until the garlic and oil begin to emulsify, about 5 to 10 minutes (this is the most important part of the process and can't be rushed; see Note). Stop at any time to scrape the garlic back into the centre of the processor if the garlic begins to build up on the sides.

Once the garlic and oil appear fluffy, pour in another tablespoon of oil and process, alternating 1 tablespoon lemon juice and 1 tablespoon oil until all of the oil and lemon juice have been added. You'll know it's done when the sauce is white and has an airy consistency like mayonnaise. The entire process will take about 10 to 15 minutes. If the mixture begins to lose volume while in the processor, do not continue to add the oil or lemon juice. Pulse the mixture until the garlic whips to a light, fluffy consistency, and then continue adding the oil and lemon juice, alternating between the two. Whipped garlic can be made up to 3 days in advance. Store in an airtight container in the refrigerator until ready to serve.

recipe continues

You will need a minimum of 1 cup garlic cloves. It seems like a lot, but the blending works only in large batches. Not to fret, this dip keeps well when chilled and it is a soul-satisfying thing to add to salads, sandwiches, burgers, and stir-fries.

Do not use anything other than canola oil, which helps lift and stabilize the garlic into a white cloud.

When you are ready to admit defeat, continue to process another 5 minutes. It will whip, I can assure you.

Prepare the Artichokes: Rinse the artichokes under cold water and pat dry. Remove the tough outer leaves until the pale-yellow, tender leaves on the inside are exposed. Use your hand to pluck off the stem of each artichoke. Trim 1 inch (2.5 cm) off the top of each artichoke and any remaining dark green bits. Halve the artichokes vertically and use a small spoon to scoop out the furry bits from the heart.

Heat a large pot of water with a steamer over high. Once the water reaches a boil, place a single layer of artichoke halves, cut side down, into the steamer. Steam the artichokes until tender, 20 to 30 minutes. The steaming time will vary based on the size of your artichokes. The artichokes are done when you can easily insert a knife into the meaty bottom half. Once done, set them in a strainer over a large bowl or the sink to drain any excess liquid. Repeat with the remaining artichoke halves.

In a large mixing bowl, combine the steamed artichokes with the olive oil and toss to coat.

Preheat a well-oiled grill over medium. Place the artichokes, cut side down, onto the grill. Grill for 6 to 8 minutes, flipping midway, until the artichokes have grill marks and effuse their intoxicating earthy scent. Season the artichokes with salt and pepper and serve with the whipped garlic. (Whipped garlic is one of the world's best defences against vampires. For those forced to socialize after eating, bring mints.)

Roasted Eggplant Dip

Makes 3 cups (750 mL)

I make this sweet and savoury dip specifically to dip chunks of hot bread into. It is a smoky, tomatoey eggplant sauce that requires little effort, and is always something I set on my table as a pre-dinner snack when hosting hot summer night gatherings.

2 large globe eggplants (each about 1 pound/450 grams)

¼ cup (60 mL) extra virgin olive oil

2 onions, chopped

¾ cup (180 mL) tomato paste

½ teaspoon kosher salt, plus more to season

Freshly cracked black pepper, to season

Fresh Italian loaf, for dipping

Preheat the oven to 350°F (175°C) and line a baking sheet with parchment paper.

Place the eggplants on the prepared baking sheet and prick each all over with a fork before they sojourn into the oven to roast until soft, about 1 hour. It's okay if the eggplant deflates like a sad balloon, this means it's ready. Give the eggplants a flip midway through the roast, at the 30-minute mark. Set the cooked eggplants in a colander in the sink to drain and cool.

As soon as the eggplants are cool enough to handle, use your hands to press the excess liquid out. Cut the eggplants in half and scoop the flesh out onto a cutting board. The peel can be discarded. Use a chef's knife to chop the flesh very finely.

In a skillet over medium, heat the oil. Once hot, add the onions and cook until soft, about 15 minutes. Add the chopped eggplant to the onions, along with the tomato paste and salt. Turn the heat to medium-low and continue to cook for 10 to 15 minutes, stirring often. If the mixture begins to stick to the skillet, add a little more oil as needed. Once the eggplant mix is glossy and tender, it has cooked through and is ready to be transferred to a bowl to cool. Taste and season with salt and pepper before serving. Serve with a fresh sliced Italian loaf for dipping. This dip can be stored in an airtight container in the refrigerator and will be just as dippable for up to 3 days.

Curly Corn Ribs with Fresh Zhoug & Shishito Peppers

Serves 4 to 6

Corn on the cob is up there in my top ten childhood food memories. In Toronto, street festival or not, chaotic city sidewalks are filled with the smell of sweet and buttery corn cobs cooking on the grill. A local summer snack that is impossible to resist, these curly corn ribs are an ode to this specialty. They're made with a simple marinade of puréed garlic, then quickly fried until they curl like the limbs of an octopus and served with cilantro-heavy zhoug: a common hot herb sauce served in Yemen, similar to chimichurri but with spices familiar to the Middle East.

Zhoug

1 cup fresh cilantro leaves

1 teaspoon ground cardamom

½ teaspoon ground cumin

4 cloves garlic

½ teaspoon kosher salt

1 shishito pepper, seeds removed and roughly chopped

¼ cup (60 mL) extra virgin olive oil

Curly Corn Ribs

4 cobs corn, husks removed

4 cloves garlic, minced to a fine purée

4 cups (1 litre) vegetable oil, for frying

2 shishito peppers (or jalapeño peppers), seeds removed and thinly sliced, for serving

1 teaspoon flaky sea salt, to season

To a mortar, add the cilantro, cardamom, cumin, garlic, and salt. Begin to grind and crush into a paste with the pestle. Add the shishito pepper and continue grinding. Lastly, pour in the olive oil and mix until a pesto-like consistency has formed. Taste before seasoning with more salt, if needed. Set aside for serving. Extra zhoug can be sealed in a jar or airtight container and stored in the refrigerator for up to 1 week.

Rub the corn cobs with the minced garlic until every crevice has been coated. Using a sharp chef's knife, cut the cobs into four quarters lengthwise (see Note). Place the corn cob "ribs" into a large bowl and set on the counter to marinate for a minimum of 1 hour.

Meanwhile, in a large, heavy pot over high, heat the vegetable oil. Once the temperature has reached 360°F (182°C), use a slotted spoon to gently submerge the corn "ribs," one at a time, in the oil (this will avoid any hot splashes). Fry a maximum of four "ribs" at a time. Fry the cobs until they begin to curl and the kernels turn golden brown, 5 to 10 minutes. Once the cobs are ready, use the same slotted spoon to remove the corn. Let the cobs drain on a paper towel–lined plate. Continue this process until all the cobs have been cooked.

Plate cobs with the thinly sliced shishito peppers and large dollops of zhoug. Finish with flaky sea salt, to taste.

NOTE: *The cobs are meant to be quartered, but if you have difficulty, then you need to get your knives sharpened. No need to risk your life; just cook them whole and fry a little longer than suggested, about 15 minutes.*

Apricot Ricotta Crostata

Serves 4

I have eaten a great many apricots in my time, and as a self-proclaimed apricot connoisseur, I will say that there is only a small window in late July to early August when you can experience the sweet succulence of a ripe apricot in Ontario. Apricots are called the "precocious ones" for a reason—they ripen quickly, which means that the only time you will taste the true flavour of an apricot in Ontario is when they are as golden-orange as the summer sun and effuse a strong, sweet smell that clings only to the apricots picked not far from home. Enjoy the peak-season Ontario apricot, while you can, with a combination of mild ingredients that will complement, rather than overpower, its flavours, as I've done here: on a pillow of mellow ricotta and drizzled with sweet honey. Simple and delicious.

4 slices fresh Italian bread

2 cups (500 mL) Fresh Ricotta
   (page 115; see Note)

¼ cup sliced raw almonds

8 small apricots, halved and stoned
   (or 4 large apricots, quartered)

2 tablespoons honey, for drizzling

Good-quality extra virgin olive oil,
   for drizzling

Flaky sea salt, to season

Toast the slices of bread in a toaster. Alternatively, preheat the oven to 300°F (150°C). Place the bread slices on a baking sheet and into the oven to cook until lightly toasted, 4 to 5 minutes.

Plate the toasts and spread ½ cup (125 mL) ricotta onto each toast. Sprinkle with sliced almonds and place an even layer of apricots onto the ricotta. Drizzle the toasts with honey and olive oil before serving. Lightly season with flaky sea salt.

NOTE: *These crostatas are best made with fresh ricotta, but if you have little time and plenty of ripe apricots, hit up your neighbourhood cheesemonger for a locally made option. If they are anything like my cheese friends at Monforte, you will have more than one delicious option to choose from.*

Caprese Frittata

Serves 4

This is my favourite way to host a brunch: serve a frittata in the very pan it was cooked, with at least one slice precut as an invitation to dig in. There is not much fuss to it. It is as simple as a whisk of all the ingredients—tiny tomatoes bobbing about—and in the oven it goes. The more pressing reason to make this is the amazing flavour of an August cherry tomato. In her ripest form, she is compact with as much sweetness as any other fruit in season, and a hint of green-vegetal flavours from the vine she grew on. Though she grew in Ontario, eating her alongside fresh basil and bocconcini feels like a warm sunny day on the island of Capri.

¼ cup grape tomatoes

6 eggs

1½ tablespoons whole milk

2 tablespoons roughly chopped sun-dried tomatoes

¼ teaspoon kosher salt

⅛ teaspoon freshly cracked black pepper

¼ cup bocconcini, torn into grape tomato–size pieces

¼ cup fresh basil, torn into bite-size pieces

Preheat the oven to 350°F (175°C).

In a deep mixing bowl, pop each grape tomato and squeeze out the juices—nobody likes a soggy frittata. (I have been known to make a tomato juice mess across my kitchen cabinets, but I have found that if I lower my hands deep enough into the bowl and gently squeeze, there is less of an explosion.) Tear a few tomatoes in half, leaving others as they are.

In a large mixing bowl, lightly beat the eggs and milk together. Add the grape tomatoes (without the juice) and sun-dried tomatoes to the egg mixture and mix together. Stir in the salt and pepper. Pour the mixture into a 4- × 13-inch (10 × 33 cm) oven-safe baking dish (10- or 12-inch/25 or 30 cm round baking dishes work too) and top with the bocconcini pieces.

Bake until the eggs set and cheese melts, give or take 15 minutes. Remove the baking dish from the oven and top the dish with the freshly torn basil leaves. Switch the oven to broil and place the dish back in the oven under the broiler for another 3 to 4 minutes (keep a close eye so as not to burn the top of the frittata). Let cool for 5 minutes before serving.

NOTE: *When serving this frittata to my non-dairy-eating friends, I switch the milk to oat milk and omit the bocconcini, but I will always set some of the latter on the side for those wary of a frittata without cheese.*

Green Tacos with Zucchini Spears

Serves 4

A trustworthy friend of mine from the northern part of Mexico once told me that corn tortillas are only to be served fresh—a tasty tidbit I have forever adopted. This meal requires a little extra effort, but fresh tortillas are worth it, I promise. The corn tortillas will assume the key task of holding your tender, grilled zucchini spears. Zucchini is at its best in August when it hits peak sweetness (later zucchini is less flavourful and has a tough exterior because the plant's energy goes to younger seeds). The summer squash will caramelize on the grill and absorb the intense flavours of the smoky salsa, fresh cilantro, and festoons of pickled red onion.

Salsa Verde

2 poblano peppers

6 tomatillos

2 cloves garlic, skin on

1 shallot, skin on

¼ cup fresh cilantro leaves

Juice of 1 lime

1 teaspoon kosher salt, plus more to season

Corn Tortillas

2 cups (250 grams) masa flour

½ teaspoon kosher salt

1½ cups (375 mL) lukewarm water, divided

For the Tacos

2 zucchinis, quartered lengthwise and halved

Kosher salt, to season

2 cups watercress

¼ cup quick pickled red onions (page 184)

¼ cup raw unsalted pumpkin seeds

1 handful fresh cilantro leaves, for garnish

1 lime, cut into wedges, for serving

Preheat a grill to high heat.

Make the Salsa Verde: Place the peppers, tomatillos, garlic cloves, and shallot onto a grill pan on the preheated grill. Grill until the skins are charred, flipping every so often to get an even char. Remove from the heat and let cool slightly so as not to burn your fingers when removing the charred bits. Remove the skins and any extra burnt pieces from the vegetable flesh. Seed the peppers and give the tomatillos and peppers a rough chop. Place the grilled vegetables, cilantro, lime juice, and salt into a mortar (or a food processor) and grind with the pestle (or pulse) into a chunky salsa. Taste and season with more salt, as needed. The salsa can be made in advance and stored in a sealed container in the refrigerator for up to 3 days.

Make the Corn Tortilla Dough: In a large mixing bowl, combine the masa flour and salt. Add 1 cup (250 mL) lukewarm water and stir until the water is absorbed. The texture will be quite crumbly. One tablespoon at a time, mix in the remaining ½ cup (125 mL) water. Once a dough has formed, continue to knead the dough in the bowl. If the dough is too sticky, add more flour. If the dough does not form into a ball, add more water. Split the dough into golf ball–size balls. The dough will make anywhere from 10 to 14 balls.

recipe continues

Cut two pieces of wax paper, each 12 inches (30 cm) square. Place one piece on a clean surface, then place your first dough ball on the wax paper. Cover with a second layer of wax paper. Press the ball with a large, flat, heavy kitchen appliance (I like to use a heavy skillet or Pyrex dish). Press down hard and evenly until the ball is ¼ inch (0.5 cm) thick. Peel the tortilla round from the paper and set aside. Repeat until all tortilla rounds are formed.

Grill the Zucchini: Season the zucchinis with salt and grill to fork-tender, about 15 minutes, flipping midway. Remove from the grill and set aside.

Cook the Corn Tortillas: Heat a non-stick skillet or comal (see Note) over medium-high. Add your first tortilla and flip immediately after 10 seconds. Cook the tortilla on one side for 1 to 2 minutes. Flip and cook for another 1 to 2 minutes, until light brown spots form on either side. Remove from the heat, stack the cooked tortillas in a clean tea towel to stay warm, and repeat the process with the remaining tortillas.

Assemble the Tacos: Place two tortillas on each plate. Spread 2 tablespoons salsa verde on each taco. Top with watercress, two zucchini spears, and ½ tablespoon pickled onions. Sprinkle with pumpkin seeds, garnish with cilantro, and serve with lime wedges.

NOTE: *The ingredients for the salsa verde require a skillet heated well past blistering—further proof that the fastest way to dinner is a grill, a cast-iron skillet, or a comal. I learned all about the comal when cooking in Mexico with someone I admire greatly, Chef Miriam Flores. For reference, it is similar to a cast-iron skillet but thinner and lighter, and is part of the magic when making fresh tortillas.*

Shaved Cucumber Salad in a Honey Sesame Dressing

Serves 2

This is a light refreshing side to whet your palate and excite your stomach for further pursuits such as sushi or, better yet, Tuna Tataki (page 132). Inspired by the Japanese sunomono salad and what is available in Ontario, these ingredients complement the ribboned cucumber. Dressed in a seasoned vinegar, the result is a very cooling, sweet healthy side that is no doubt a dish for the eyes and very easy to prepare.

Honey Sesame Dressing

2 tablespoons rice vinegar

2 tablespoons good-quality extra virgin olive oil

1 tablespoon sesame oil

1 tablespoon honey

Kosher salt, to season

1 English cucumber, shaved into thin ribbons

1 tablespoon mix of black and white sesame seeds

2 tablespoons quick pickled onions (optional; see page 184)

Edible flowers (like pansies, cilantro flowers, nasturtiums, or chamomiles), for garnish (optional)

In a large mixing bowl, whisk together the vinegar, olive oil, sesame oil, and honey. Season with salt to taste. Submerge the cucumber ribbons in the dressing and let marinate for 15 minutes.

Gently plate the cucumber ribbons. Sprinkle with the sesame seeds. Top with the pickled onions and edible flowers, if desired, right before serving.

Tuna Tataki with Shichimi Togarashi
Serves 4

Have you ever had one of those moments when you experience a new food and from then on out, your views on food change? That is tuna tataki for me. Specifically at Guu Izakaya, Toronto's first izakaya. There are plenty of izakayas in the city where you can try this wonderful dish, though sometimes I like to make it myself. Tuna tataki is not quite raw like sashimi, but rather is lightly seared in a trifecta of seasoning: spicy, citrusy, and earthy. Warm and crunchy on the outside but cool and buttery on the inside. I will always wait until the last minute to remove the fish from the refrigerator—I love the contrast in temperatures. It takes less than ten minutes to prepare and suits busy days to appease my voracious appetite. Serve on a bed of salad, like Shaved Cucumber Salad in a Honey Sesame Dressing (page 131).

½ pound (225 grams) sashimi-grade tuna (see Note), stored in the refrigerator

Kosher salt, to season

Shichimi Togarashi *(see Note)*

½ tablespoon dried chili flakes

½ tablespoon ground sumac

1 tablespoon hemp seeds

1 tablespoon kelp flakes

1 tablespoon poppy seeds

2 tablespoons grapeseed oil

Lightly season all sides of the tuna with salt. (Pre-salt for an extra flavourful and tender fish.) Return the tuna to the refrigerator to keep cool until ready to use.

In a small bowl, mix the chili flakes, sumac, hemp seeds, kelp flakes, and poppy seeds together.

Spread the shichimi togarashi on a piece of wax or parchment paper. Remove the tuna from the refrigerator and lay one side on top of the shichimi togarashi. Turn and pat each side of the tuna into the shichimi togarashi until the tuna is fully covered.

In a large skillet over high, heat the oil. Once the skillet is very hot, use tongs to add the crusted tuna. Sear each side for 1 to 3 minutes. The outside should be lightly browned and crispy while the inside remains cool and pink. Once all sides, including the edges, are seared, remove from the heat and let sit for 5 minutes before cutting into slices. Cut the tuna against the grain, to keep the slices extra tender.

NOTES

Shichimi togarashi can be found in most supermarkets nowadays, so you can purchase it instead of making your own.

It's always worth looking at seafoodwatch.org for the most sustainable tuna option.

Herbed Wrapped Rainbow Trout

Serves 8

This meal involves little more than the slicing of a few vegetables and salting a fish. A light meal with fresh herbs and little preparation is what I consider a perfect summer dish. There is a lemon to zest, a couple of garlic cloves to mince, and the rest is an assembly job. Get yourself some good kitchen twine and feel free to go wild with whatever herbs you have on hand—at this time of year, every herb is in season, they all are delicious, and really anything will go well with trout. I like to serve the flaky, herb-flecked centrepiece with a side of seasonal vegetables—zucchini, eggplant, corn, string beans, and onions boasting grill marks.

---

1 whole trout (1½ pounds/ 680 grams), prepared for stuffing (see Note)

Fine sea salt

3 tablespoons (45 mL) extra virgin olive oil, divided

½ cup ground cherries (see Note, page 76)

Freshly cracked black pepper

2 lemons, 1 sliced and 1 zested and juiced, divided

2 shallots, thinly sliced

1 fennel (1 pound/450 grams), cut paper-thin (see Note)

2 cloves garlic, minced

1 handful fresh herbs, like fennel fronds, rosemary, thyme, and chives

Preheat the oven to 450°F (230°C) and line a baking sheet with parchment paper.

Season the entire trout with a generous amount of salt, so that an even layer of salt coats both the outside and the cavity of the fish.

In a medium mixing bowl, combine 2 tablespoons olive oil with the ground cherries and toss to coat. Season with salt and pepper.

Place the trout on the prepared baking sheet. Rub the outside of the fish with the remaining 1 tablespoon oil and season with pepper. Stuff the cavity of the fish with the lemon slices, shallots, fennel, garlic, and herbs. Sprinkle the ground cherries around the fish, and if you have extra fresh herbs, spread them around the fish too. Roast the fish until the flesh is opaque, about 20 minutes. Remove from the heat and set aside to cool for 5 minutes before serving with a garnish of fresh lemon zest and juice.

NOTES

Rainbow trout is a known trout of the Great Lakes and listed as a responsible option on seafoodwatch.org. Trout bought at a fishmonger, prepared for stuffing, comes deboned, so this is not something you will have to worry about doing yourself.

When cutting vegetables paper-thin, I like to use my kitchen staple: the vegetable peeler. A mandoline works just as well too.

Apricot BBQ Sticky Ribs

Serves 6

The popularity and excellent PR of an August peach has cast a shadow on the poor apricot, which makes me believe that apricots are the most underrated fruit of Ontario. Not only wonderful eaten fresh from the market but in a sticky barbecue sauce, an apricot will bring out the best of these grilled rib's smoky flavours (which may have gone barely noticed otherwise). Always, always, always pick a good-quality meat; your ribs will be as good as the farm the animals were raised on. I like to serve my ribs with a side of potatoes made however my guests like them (you could go with the Crispy Smashed Potatoes on page 50 or the Crispy Homemade Fries on page 256). If you have time, marinate these ribs 1 day ahead of grilling—that 24 hours will make them even better.

---

4 pounds (1.8 kilograms) beef back ribs

Kosher salt, to season

Sticky Apricot BBQ Sauce

4 ripe apricots, stoned and roughly chopped

½ cup (125 mL) extra virgin olive oil

¼ cup (60 mL) canola oil

2 cloves garlic, minced

¼ cup (60 mL) honey

3 tablespoons Dijon mustard

3 tablespoons balsamic vinegar

½ teaspoon kosher salt

Freshly cracked black pepper, to season

Season the ribs with salt and place evenly across a shallow baking dish.

Place the apricots, olive and canola oils, garlic, honey, mustard, balsamic vinegar, salt, and pepper into a blender and blend on high until a smooth sauce has formed. Pour the sauce over the ribs in the baking dish. Cover the dish and marinate the ribs for 6 to 24 hours in the refrigerator.

Preheat a well-oiled grill to 250°F (120°C). Wipe excess marinade off the ribs. Close the grill and cook the ribs for 1 hour and 20 minutes, flipping every 20 minutes (and with an internal temperature of 160°F/71°C; see Note). Transfer the ribs to a cutting board, tent with foil, and let rest for 5 minutes before serving.

NOTE: *The only accurate way to check when your ribs are done is checking their internal temperature with an instant-read thermometer. Ribs are safe to eat at any point after 160°F (71°C) but will be fall-off-the-bone at 190°F (88°C).*

Blackberry Nectarine Crisp

Serves 6

I often look at dessert as a way to dress up my favourite fruit. This crisp is a great excuse to fold plump berries and smooth stone fruit together, baked softly into a crumbly crust of spices, butter, and sugar. I've done my best to keep things simple here and let the ingredients (and fruit!) speak for themselves, with little else to interfere. Thyme can be an unconventional choice in dessert, but there is a peppery and minty quality to it that complements a tart earthy blackberry very well. You will need a large spoon to serve this crisp while still warm and bubbling, and it is even better with a scoop of cool vanilla ice cream to make for a delightful summer evening.

Crisp Topping

½ cup (64 grams) all-purpose flour (or almond flour)

½ cup (50 grams) old-fashioned rolled oats

½ cup (105 grams) firmly packed brown sugar

¼ teaspoon ground cinnamon

2 tablespoons fresh thyme leaves

¼ teaspoon kosher salt

6 tablespoons (90 grams) cold unsalted butter, diced

Berry Nectarine Filling

4 cups pitted and sliced nectarines (½-inch/1 cm slices)

¼ cup (60 mL) honey

1 tablespoon arrowroot starch (or organic corn starch)

½ teaspoon pure vanilla extract

1 cup blackberries

Vanilla ice cream, for serving (optional)

Preheat the oven to 375°F (190°C).

In the bowl of a food processor, combine the flour, oats, brown sugar, cinnamon, thyme, and salt and pulse twice to mix. Add the cold butter to the flour mixture and pulse a few more times until the mixture forms small crumbles. Alternatively, if you are not feeling up for pulling out the food processor, place the flour, oats, brown sugar, cinnamon, thyme, and salt in a large bowl and use a large spoon or your hands to mix until well incorporated. Add the diced cold butter and continue to mix with your hands until you have formed a crumbly dough. Set aside.

In a large mixing bowl, combine the nectarines, honey, arrowroot starch, and vanilla. Pour the fruit mixture into a 5- × 9-inch (12 × 23 cm) loaf pan. Scatter the blackberries on top of the nectarines and sprinkle with the crisp topping. Bake until the fruit begins to bubble and the crumble on top is golden, 45 to 60 minutes. Serve warm with vanilla ice cream, if desired.

Dutch Baby with Stewed Rosemary Blueberries

Serves 4

Native to Ontario in their wild form, blueberries are teeny little gems with plenty of amusement for the palate. When markets are packed with blueberry stalls from July through to August, you have plenty of opportunity to try a delicately sweet true-to-Ontario fruit. If you look closely, you will notice a silver coating on a blueberry—that is there to protect them, so wash only when you are ready to eat them. Though they are quite spirited on their own, a little rosemary can heighten the flavours of the blueberry with its lemon-pine pungency, making for two nice partners, especially when served on a puffy Dutch baby pancake.

Stewed Rosemary Blueberries

1 cup blueberries

1 tablespoon water

1 tablespoon granulated sugar

1 sprig rosemary (or 1 teaspoon dried)

Dutch Baby

½ cup (65 grams) all-purpose flour

½ cup (125 mL) oat milk (or any milk)

3 eggs

2 tablespoons granulated sugar

½ teaspoon kosher salt

2 tablespoons (30 grams) unsalted butter, room temperature

In a medium skillet over medium-high, heat the blueberries and water. Once the liquid begins to form little bubbles, reduce the heat to medium-low and add the sugar and rosemary. Stir and stew until the sugar has dissolved, 2 minutes. Remove from the heat and set the stewed rosemary blueberries aside, removing any woody stems of rosemary.

In a blender or food processor fitted with the blade attachment, place the flour, milk, eggs, sugar, and salt. Blend for 10 seconds, scrape down the sides, and then blend for another 10 seconds. The batter will be quite loose (like a liquid). Allow the batter to rest in the blender for 20 to 25 minutes. This will give the flour a chance to absorb the liquid and the batter to thicken.

Meanwhile, preheat the oven to 425°F (220°C). Place a 12-inch (30 cm) oven-safe skillet in the oven to warm along with the oven. When the batter has finished resting, remove the skillet from the oven (remember, it will be hot, so use oven mitts). Add the butter and swirl the pan to melt the butter and coat the bottom and sides of the pan. Pour the batter into the butter-coated skillet and tilt the pan to spread the batter evenly across all sides of the skillet.

Bake until the Dutch baby has puffed into a golden cloud with darker brown, crispy edges, 15 to 20 minutes. Serve hot from the pan and top with your stewed rosemary blueberries.

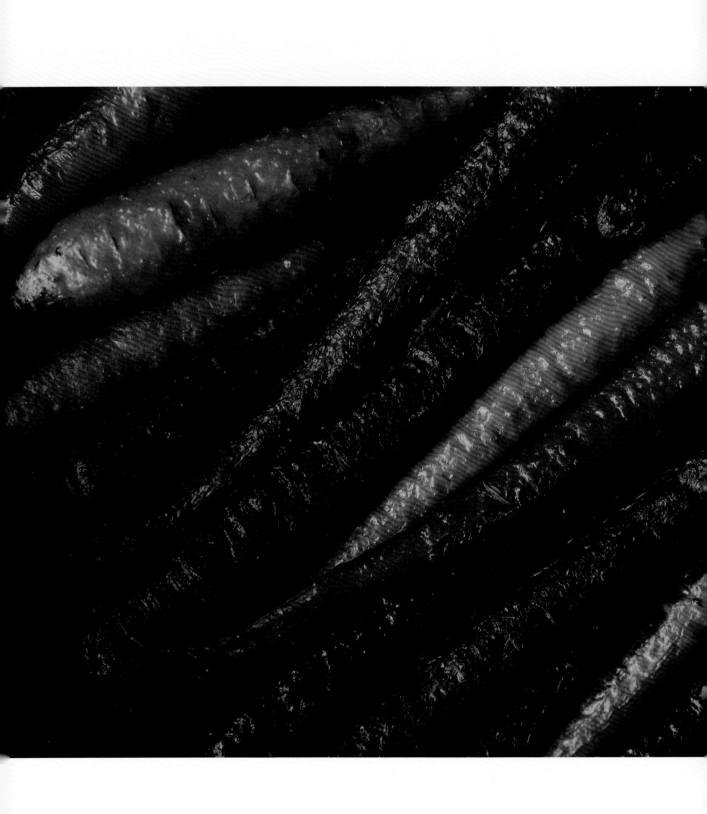

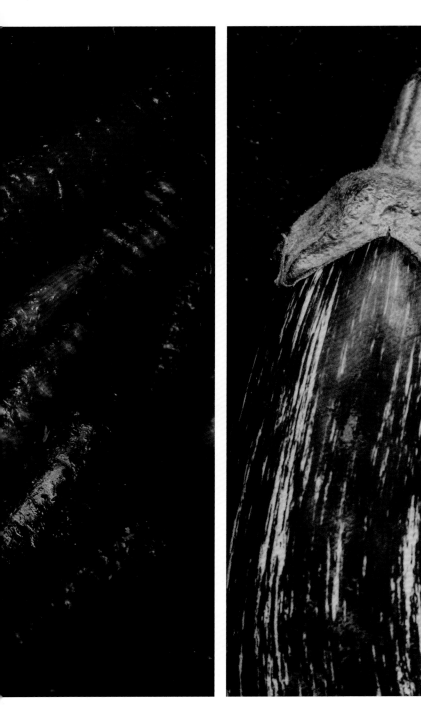
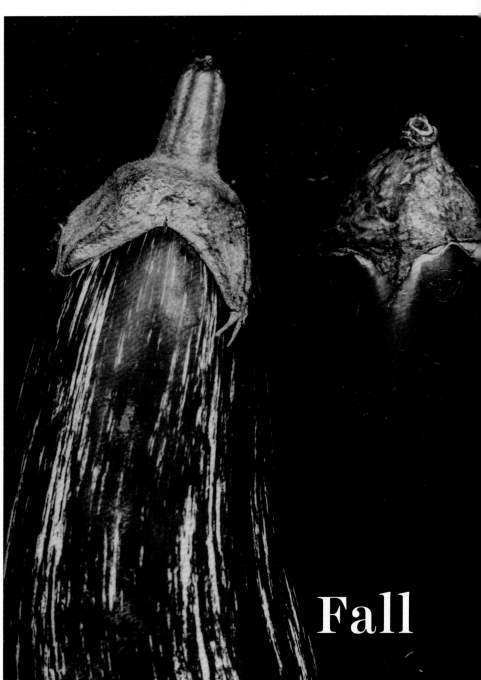

Fall

FALL IS A SPECIAL MOMENT when what was planted in the spring and left in the soil for months to grow finally emerges. Late potatoes, sunchokes, Ukrainian garlic, Romanesco broccoli, purple daikon, and Brussels sprouts all appear at the market, as do fairy tale eggplants and heirloom tomatoes. The abundance of summer vegetables and fruits still linger and there is a time of overlap when you can have a Field Tomato Salad with Herb & Garlic Oil (page 152) on the same day you make Apple Cider Doughnuts (page 146).

And then the leaves drop and the air cools. With the whirlwind of summer behind us, we can all take a breath and savour the beginning of a slower season. Scarves and teacups are spotted on the streets, and I find myself making large turkey roast dinners for family, served with the standard fall celebrities like Sunchoke, Cauliflower & Leek Soup with Canadian Gremolata (page 168) or Roasted Delicata Squash with Sage Salsa Verde (page 172), and we relish in the last of summer's sweets with a Plum Port Tart (page 180). Part of the market's charm in the fall is to see the delicate leaves of warm weather arugula share a table with a heavy, thick-skinned acorn squash. It is a milieu to welcome hardy cool crops into our homes and bid adieu to the last of summer's delights.

How To: Make Apple Cider Doughnuts

Makes 10 to 12 doughnuts

There are two classic types of doughnut: the yeasted doughnut and the cake doughnut. For this recipe, I've chosen the latter, as its crispy edges and soft cake interior picks up the flavour of apple cider better than its airy counterpart. And there is no better way to embrace the cooling temperatures than with the quintessential warming cinnamon and apples of the fall. It is the McIntosh apple—a variety conceived in Upper Canada that is distinctively used to make products like apple cider and apple sauce—that gives these doughnuts their strong apple flavour. There is a bit of work involved in making these, but I have provided a step-by-step guide to help you through the baking process. I wouldn't get too hung up on perfection here, and don't be concerned about looks—the craggier the doughnut, the more flavour it will pick up (while providing a lesson on appreciating the beauty of imperfections).

Equipment

1 medium pot

1 or 2 large mixing bowls

1 stand-up mixer or handheld mixer

2 baking sheets

2 pieces parchment paper (each 12 × 20 inches/30 × 50 cm), plus more for the baking sheets

1 rolling pin

1 pastry brush

1 large round pastry cutter (2½ to 4½ inches/6 to 11 cm) (or a wide-mouth tumbler)

1 small round pastry cutter (¾ inch/2 cm) (or the top of a wine bottle)

2 shallow mixing bowls

Make the Dough

Step 1: In a medium pot over high heat, bring the apple cider to a boil and cook until the cider has reduced to ⅓ cup (80 mL) and looks like thin honey, 15 to 20 minutes. Set aside to cool to room temperature, about 10 minutes.

Step 2: In a large mixing bowl, combine the flour, baking powder, baking soda, salt, cinnamon, and cream of tartar. Mix until everything is well incorporated.

Step 3: In a stand-up mixer fitted with the paddle attachment or a large mixing bowl with a hand mixer, beat the room-temperature butter for 30 seconds on low speed. Slowly add in the sugar as you continue to beat, gradually increasing the speed to high, until the texture is a sticky clay, 1 to 2 minutes. Mix in the eggs and give everything a good mix, until well incorporated. Add the apple sauce and cooled apple cider reduction and give it one more good mix before pouring the wet ingredients into the dry ingredients. Mix until thoroughly combined and there are no dry spots remaining. The dough should be like a moist batter. Cover the dough and set in the refrigerator to cool for 1 hour.

Apple Cider Doughnuts

1 cup (250 mL) apple cider, plus a little more for brushing (see Note)

3 cups (400 grams) gluten-free flour blend (see Note) or all-purpose flour

1 tablespoon baking powder

½ tablespoon baking soda

1 teaspoon kosher salt

1 teaspoon ground cinnamon

½ teaspoon cream of tartar

⅓ cup (80 grams) unsalted butter, room temperature

¾ cup (150 grams) granulated sugar (see Note)

2 eggs

⅓ cup (80 mL) unsweetened apple sauce

Cinnamon Sugar Topping

¼ cup (60 mL) unsalted butter, melted

½ cup (100 grams) granulated sugar

½ teaspoon ground cinnamon

⅛ teaspoon kosher salt

Bake the Doughnuts

Step 4: Preheat the oven to 375°F (190°C) and line two baking sheets with parchment paper.

Cut two pieces of parchment paper and place one on a clean surface. Dust this parchment paper with a layer of flour, then add the chilled dough, giving it an extra dusting of flour, and top with the second piece of parchment paper. With a rolling pin, gently roll out the dough between the floured pieces of paper into a ½-inch (1 cm) thick rectangle. Grab both ends of the parchment papers and flip the dough. Remove the top parchment paper and, with a dry pastry brush, lightly sweep away excess flour. Cut as many doughnuts and holes as possible. (I use a 4½-inch/11 cm wide-mouth tumbler coated in flour for the doughnut shape, but a 2½-inch/6 cm round cutter is great if you have one on hand. The top of a clean, lightly floured wine bottle is perfect for cutting the doughnut hole, but you can also use a ¾-inch/2 cm cutter.) The scraps can be combined, rerolled, and cut until all the dough is used up. Place the cut doughnuts on the prepared baking sheets and brush each doughnut with a bit of extra apple cider. Bake for 18 to 20 minutes or until a toothpick inserted into the centre comes out clean. Let the doughnuts cool slightly—enough to handle but still warm—before topping with cinnamon sugar (see below).

Top with Cinnamon Sugar

Step 5: While the doughnuts are cooling, prepare two shallow bowls: one with the melted butter and the second with a well-combined mixture of the sugar, cinnamon, and salt. Once the doughnuts are cool enough to handle, take one and dip all edges in the butter, lift to remove any excess drippings, and dip into the cinnamon sugar. Set aside and repeat with all remaining doughnuts.

These doughnuts are best eaten fresh (and warm) but, if need be, can be sealed in a container and enjoyed slightly drier the next day with a warm cup of coffee to dip in.

recipe continues

NOTES

Apple cider is at its best in the fall from a local farmers' market, but you can also find the good, perishable, cloudy cider in the refrigerator section of your local supermarket. It's much more flavourful than the clear apple beverages on the shelf.

Gluten-free flour can be store-bought or you can make it yourself. For this recipe, combine 1 cup almond flour (95 grams), 1 cup sorghum flour (140 grams), and 1 cup potato starch (150 grams).

Maple syrup is a nice substitute for the granulated sugar, but will not yield a cake doughnut as fluffy and moist as sugar does.

Broccolini in Chili Garlic Oil with Crushed Caramel Peanuts

Serves 4

I have an affinity for the bitterness of broccoli's little sister—broccolini—and when cooked in garlic oil, this dish is taken to the next level, with the garlic amplifying the savoury, spicy, and sweet flavour profiles of the ingredients. The additional caramel crunch of candied peanuts counterbalances the sharp, pungent greens, finishing off the dish beautifully. Much like broccoli, broccolini is in peak season from summer through to fall, so you can make this dish anytime. I have yet to decide if this is a side to a heavy pasta or hardy meal or a fantastic dessert to serve on its own. I will let you see for yourself.

---

3 tablespoons extra virgin olive oil

4 cloves garlic, minced

1 teaspoon dried chili flakes

2 bunches broccolini (8 to 14 stalks), woody ends removed

2 tablespoons pure maple syrup

½ cup raw peanuts, halved

Juice of 1 lemon

Kosher salt and freshly cracked black pepper, to season

Good-quality extra virgin olive oil, for drizzling

In a large skillet over medium-high, heat the olive oil. Add the garlic and reduce heat to medium. Cook, stirring often, until fragrant, 1 to 2 minutes. Add the chili flakes, give everything a good stir, then add the broccolini. Stirring every so often, cook until wilted, 8 to 10 minutes. Remove the garlicky broccolini from the skillet and set aside on a plate.

Reduce the heat to medium-low and add the syrup and peanuts. Cook for 3 minutes. Remove the skillet from the heat and let the caramel peanuts rest for 5 minutes.

Drizzle the lemon juice over the broccolini and season with a generous pinch of salt and pepper. Drizzle with the olive oil and sprinkle with the caramel peanuts to serve.

Field Tomato Salad with Herb & Garlic Oil

Serves 4

No amount of year-round greenhouse-grown tomatoes can compare to a field tomato warmed by the late summer and early autumn sun. Its savouriness (umami) is in its DNA—a perfect balance of sweet and acerbic that needs nothing more than salt. But now and then, I like to add a few extra aromatics and a drizzle of oil to turn a few perfect tomatoes into one handsome salad.

2 tablespoons good-quality extra virgin olive oil

2 cloves garlic, thinly sliced

1 tablespoon white wine vinegar

2 tablespoons fresh oregano leaves

2 pounds (900 grams) mixed field tomatoes, sliced ¼ inch (0.5 cm) thick

½ teaspoon flaky sea salt or finishing salt

In a small skillet over low, heat the oil. Add the sliced garlic and increase the heat to medium-low to infuse the oil. Cook until the garlic is golden, 10 to 15 minutes. Remove from the heat and set aside for the dressing.

In a small mixing bowl, whisk together the garlic-infused olive oil, vinegar, and oregano. Set aside the dressing for serving.

Arrange the tomatoes on a plate, drizzle with the dressing, and season with salt. Serve and enjoy immensely.

Soft Baked Eggplant with Crispy Millet, Calabrese Peppers & Honey-Almond Drizzle

Serves 4

So many types of eggplant varieties are available in September, and I highly recommend playing around with the different shapes and sizes you come across. I love the striped look of graffiti eggplants, the long, thin Japanese eggplants, and, of course, the large meaty globe variety. The last is the most commonly available, and it works in this recipe when serving a few extra-hungry folks; you will just need to slice it a few extra times for accurate cook time. Using a few different types of eggplant can make for a beautiful presentation, and all types, once roasted, are a fine match for the sweet and nutty honey-almond drizzle, the spicy kick of the Calabrese peppers, and the fresh citrus zings of parsley and sumac. Millet adds a nice chew and a bit of sustenance, making this a hardy lunch or a substantial side.

1½ cups (375 mL) water

½ cup millet, rinsed (see Note)

2 cloves garlic, minced

Flaky sea salt, to season

1 tablespoon honey (see Note)

2 tablespoons good-quality extra virgin olive oil, plus 1 teaspoon to coat the baking sheet

4 tablespoons almond butter

4 small (Japanese, graffiti, or fairy tale) or 2 medium (globe) eggplants

½ cup roughly chopped Calabrese peppers in oil (see Note)

1 teaspoon ground sumac

¼ cup flat-leaf parsley leaves, roughly torn

In a small pot over high, bring the water to a boil. Reduce the heat to medium-low. Add the millet and garlic to the boiling water. Simmer until the millet is fluffy and fully cooked, 20 to 25 minutes. Remove the pot from the heat and fluff the millet with a fork. Season with salt and set aside.

In a small mixing bowl, whisk together the honey, 2 tablespoons olive oil, and almond butter. Season with salt.

Preheat the oven to 375°F (190°C) and lightly coat the baking sheet with the remaining teaspoon of olive oil.

If using small eggplants, cut them in half. If using larger eggplants, slice them into ½-inch (1 cm) pieces lengthwise. Score the flesh of the eggplant diagonally four to five times. Season with salt and set aside to rest while the oven preheats. Place the eggplants, cut side up, on the prepared baking sheet. Bake until fork-tender, 15 to 20 minutes (if using small eggplants) or 25 to 30 minutes (if using medium eggplants). Set aside on a serving plate to cool, but keep the oven on.

Once the eggplants are cooled, spread the almond drizzle across each slice. Evenly divide the cooked millet across each slice and top with a sprinkling of Calabrese peppers, ground sumac, and parsley.

NOTES

Millet is a tiny, gluten-free grain from the grass family. It is quick to cook and very nutritious, especially compared with the other major cereals, like wheat and rice. The most common type grown in Ontario is proso millet—nutty with a similar fluffy texture to perfectly steamed rice.

I recommend picking a local honey instead of your standard superstore honey. Local honey helps improve seasonal allergies and is often fresher than the latter. I use a wildflower honey from a friend, Irina from Bees Universe. Different honeys will change this dish slightly, but it is really up to you if you'd like to add a hint of floral, fruit, or earth to your dish.

You can find Italian Calabrese peppers in oil at most Italian grocery shops and at some superstores. If you can't find them, I recommend using oil-soaked roasted red peppers with ½ teaspoon dried chili flakes instead.

Crispy Salmon on Cantaloupe Ribbons & Salty Potato Crisps
Serves 4

Cantaloupe is always last to be eaten and never fawned over at my family's table. Still, it would be inaccurate—and frankly inadequate—to consider the melon a lowly filler in fruit salad. It would be more accurate to say that cantaloupe takes a back seat to no fruit, and this sweet and salty dish makes a strong case for that—especially at the end of summer and beginning of fall, when cantaloupes are in peak season—extra juicy, extra sweet—in Ontario. For best results, opt for a thick cut of skin-on salmon (I like to use seafoodwatch.org for ever-changing sustainable options). Use your senses and adjust your cook time depending on the thickness of the fillet. You are looking for a tender, flaky salmon with a crisp bacon-like skin.

Salty Potato Crisps

2 pounds (900 grams) Yukon Gold potatoes, sliced paper-thin

¼ cup (60 mL) extra virgin olive oil

½ teaspoon kosher salt

Flaky sea salt, to season

Crispy Salmon

4 skin-on salmon fillets (each 4 ounces/110 grams)

Kosher salt and freshly cracked black pepper

4 tablespoons all-purpose flour

4 tablespoons extra virgin olive oil

¼ cantaloupe, ribboned paper-thin with a vegetable peeler or mandoline (about 4 cups)

Preheat the oven to 400°F (200°C) and line two large baking sheets with parchment paper.

In a large mixing bowl, toss the potato slices with the oil and kosher salt until well coated. Spread the potato slices evenly across the prepared baking sheets. Keep little pockets of space between each potato slice to achieve the perfect golden crisp on each slice. Bake until most potatoes are golden around the edges, 20 to 30 minutes, flipping midway. Season with flaky sea salt as desired.

Season both sides of each salmon fillet with salt and pepper. To achieve crispier skin, lightly dust the skin side of each fillet with flour. Heat a large cast-iron skillet or oven-safe skillet over high heat. Add the oil. Once the oil is shimmering, reduce the heat to medium and add the salmon fillets, skin side down. Cook for 4 minutes, gently pressing the fish with a flexible spatula just long enough to ensure the skin is making good contact with the skillet. Spoon extra skillet oil over the top of the fish as it cooks. Cook until the skin easily lifts from the pan without resistance. Once all the fillets have crispy skins, transfer the skillet to the oven and roast until the fish is flaky and tender (1-inch/2.5 cm thick salmon takes 10 to 12 minutes).

Transfer the fish to rest on a paper towel–lined plate for 5 minutes before serving. Serve on a plate of the sweet cantaloupe ribbons with a side of the salty potato crisps.

Prosciutto Pear Pizza with Fresh Buffalo Mozzarella

Makes one 12-inch (30 cm) pizza

Note: This recipe needs to be prepared 24 hours in advance, and you will need a kitchen scale.

There are many ways to make a pizza, but this is the one I am loyal to and it always yields a good result with nothing more than a kitchen oven. The crust comes out Neapolitan-style—a thin, pillowy chew with a slightly thicker and crisp edge. The simple base is one that can support the layers of creamy mozzarella, salty prosciutto, fresh arugula, and sweet, seasonal pear.

1 pizza (page 97, steps 1 to 5; see Note)

3 tablespoons extra virgin olive oil

2 cloves garlic, minced

½ firm pear (Bosc, if available), cored and finely sliced (see Note)

2 ounces (60 grams) prosciutto, divided

½ cup arugula

3 ounces (85 grams) fresh buffalo mozzarella, torn

The day before you'd like to eat your pizza, make the pizza dough (page 97, steps 1 and 2). The next day, finish preparing the dough and par-bake it (page 98, steps 3 to 5). To finish the pizza, ensure that your oven is heated to 475°F (250°C).

Evenly spread the oil and garlic around the par-baked pizza. Top with the pear and prosciutto. Hold off on adding arugula and torn buffalo mozzarella; it's best to add these once the pizza has been cooked through. Bake the pizza on the centre rack of the oven until the pear lightly browns and the crust achieves your desired crispness, 15 minutes or so (see Note). Top with arugula and buffalo mozzarella. Slice and serve.

NOTES

Making your own dough requires preparation the night before serving the pizza. If you don't have time, skip this step but find a good bakery where you can source quality dough.

Pick a firm pear, like a Bosc, that holds up nicely when cooked. Boscs are the oblong green-brown type with a shelf life so good that when picked at summer's end, they can last through the winter.

Every oven is different, so keep a close eye during the last minutes of the bake. A lot of effort and love went into this—you wouldn't want your entire pizza to burn.

NOTE: *Hazelnuts grow in Ontario. They mature in September and are harvested for the following 6 weeks. The tree they grow on is called a hazel tree (which I think is a fantastic name). When you see a newly harvested nut, it will be encased in its beautiful bright green and blush pink leaves, making it look more like a bud of an ornamental flower.*

Chocolate Hazelnut Semifreddo

Serves 8

A semifreddo is the perfect way to cool down on still-hot September nights—a welcome occurrence. It's fluffy and sliceable and can be considered the lazy cook's ice cream. Don't let that stop you from appreciating the elegance of the silky chocolate ganache folded into cream and hazelnuts that completely adulterate its airy lightness. I like to serve this with a cup of coffee to bring out as much of the chocolate flavour as possible.

Chocolate Hazelnut Ganache

½ cup (125 mL) heavy cream

½ cup (70 grams) roughly chopped roasted hazelnuts

8.8 ounces (250 grams) 70% dark chocolate, roughly chopped

¼ teaspoon kosher salt

Semifreddo

3 cups (750 mL) water

3 eggs

2 egg yolks

½ cup (60 grams) powdered sugar, sifted

2 teaspoons pure vanilla extract

Pinch of kosher salt

1½ cups (375 mL) heavy cream

Line a 5- × 9-inch (12 × 23 cm) loaf pan with wax paper.

In a small saucepan over medium, heat the cream to a boil. Remove from the heat and add the hazelnuts, chocolate, and salt. Set aside for 2 minutes. Stir until the chocolate has melted completely. Pour the ganache into the prepared loaf pan, give the pan a gentle tap on the counter to get an even layer of ganache across the pan, then set the ganache aside to cool to room temperature.

In a saucepan over high, bring the water to a boil. Reduce the heat to medium-low and let simmer. Place the eggs, egg yolks, powdered sugar, vanilla, and salt in a heatproof bowl and set over the simmering saucepan. Use a handheld electric mixer to beat the egg mixture until thickened, 6 minutes. Remove the egg mixture from the heat and beat for another 6 minutes, until cooled.

In a medium mixing bowl, whisk the cream to soft peaks, 6 to 8 minutes. By the 4-minute mark, you may think you are ready and can skip the remaining 2 to 4 minutes, but do not stop! Semifreddo is made up of 50% air, so continue until you reach a thick mousse. Gently fold the cream through the egg mixture until well combined. Pour the cream and egg mixture over the ganache, seal with a lid or plastic wrap, and freeze for 4 to 6 hours or until firm.

To serve, remove the semifreddo from the freezer and let sit for 5 to 10 minutes to soften slightly before slicing and eating. (Softening time will depend on the time of year and how hot your kitchen is. The semifreddo should still be cold, but soft enough to slice a butter knife through with ease.) Semifreddo can last in the freezer, well wrapped, for up to 7 days; however, changing the dessert's temperature more than once can result in undesired ice crystals.

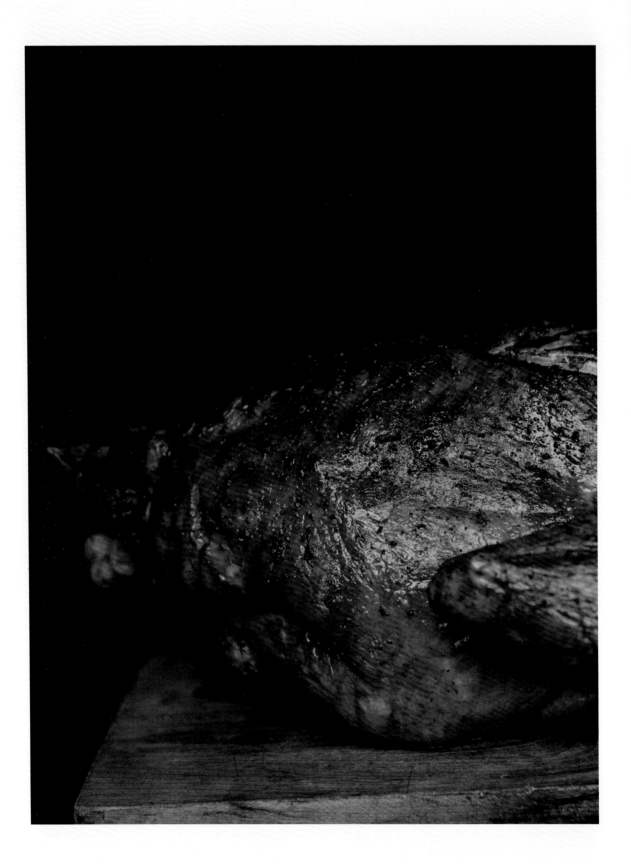

How To: Roast a Turkey

Serves 8

October generally calls for a dinner table groaning under the weight of autumn delights, with many of us celebrating Thanksgiving. It begins with a succulent turkey. The main choices when raising (or eating) livestock are breed, feed, and environment. I prefer heritage turkeys, like Artisan Gold, because they thrive in a free-range environment. Not everyone can access these turkeys, and that is okay because no matter what turkey you bring home, as long as you give the bird a good salting 1 to 2 days prior to roasting, the dry brine will keep any meat juicy and will help deliver a beautifully crisp, browned skin. I suggest never skimping on the aromatics or butter—one hour in and the scents of warm rosemary and garlic will entice even the non-turkey eaters.

Equipment

1 medium mixing bowl

1 roasting pan (14 × 17 inches/ 36 × 43 cm) with a V-shape roasting rack

1 small saucepan

1 turkey baster

1 instant-read thermometer

Turkey

¾ cup (100 grams) kosher salt

3 tablespoons honey

1 turkey (12 pounds/5.4 kilograms), neck and giblets removed (see Note)

½ cup (120 grams) unsalted butter, divided

2 sprigs rosemary

2 cloves garlic, crushed

Step 1: Place the salt and honey in a medium bowl and work together with a spatula until well mixed. You may not need all of this dry brine, but it is nice to have extra when some may end up on the roasting pan as you season the turkey.

Step 2: Place the turkey on a V-shape roasting rack set inside a large roasting pan. Rub the brine over the turkey, inside and out—make sure to wedge some into areas where the skin naturally separates from the bird, such as around the neck and top of the breast and between the legs and breast. Chill, uncovered, at least 12 hours and up to 2 days.

Step 3: Prepare the bird for roasting. Working from the neck side, wiggle your fingers under the skin to spread ¼ cup butter evenly over both breasts. In a small saucepan over medium-low, melt the remaining ¼ cup butter with the rosemary and garlic, and cook until bubbling and fragrant, about 5 minutes; keep warm. Smear the outside of the turkey with the aromatic melted butter. Ensure the turkey is breast side up on the rack before roasting in the roasting pan. If the wings are not already tucked in, tuck them in and pour 1 cup (250 mL) water into the bottom of the pan to prevent drippings from burning. Cover with foil (see Note for sustainable alternative) and let the turkey sit at room temperature for 2 hours before roasting.

recipe continues

Step 4: Set an oven rack in the lower third of the oven and preheat to 450°F (230°C).

Step 5: Roast the turkey. Midway through the roast (about 90 minutes in for a 12-pound/5.4-kilogram bird), add more water (1½ cups/ 375 mL) to the bottom of the pan and rotate the pan back to front. Roast until the skin is golden brown all over, another 35 to 45 minutes.

Step 6: Reduce the oven temperature to 350°F (175°C) and continue to roast the turkey, basting with the butter drippings every 10 to 15 minutes and rotating the pan after about 30 minutes at this temperature. Your turkey is ready once the skin is deep golden brown, shiny, and crisp (about 3 hours for a 12-pound/5.4-kilogram bird). An instant-read thermometer inserted into the thickest part of the breast near the neck should register 150°F (66°C) (the temperature will continue to climb to about 170° F/77°C while the bird rests). Let rest for 1 hour before transferring to a cutting board to carve and serve.

NOTES

Before preparing your turkey, reach inside the turkey cavity and remove the neck and giblets. These can be reserved for making a gravy or broth (see page 248).

Instead of using foil, try covering the turkey with large leaves of lacinato kale. So long as the turkey is completely covered, this will protect the skin from burning and result in crispy turkey-flavoured kale chips!

Farmer Eggs & Maitake on a Bed of Wild Black Rice & Beluga Lentils

Serves 4

The maitake mushroom—also affably named hen-of-the-woods and technically called a Grifola fron-dosa, which sounds very much like an elf queen in The Lord of the Rings—*has a woodsy flavour to it. These mushrooms are wavy, brown clusters akin to a chicken with ruffled feathers. I like to treat the hen-of-the-woods like a piece of meat: both are savoury and can be a bit pricey. But certain times of the year at the market, if you are lucky, a farmer may give you a friendly deal. When sautéed, the maitake takes on a malty, caramel flavour that is only complemented by the bed of wild black rice and beluga lentils it rests on in this dish. Both the rice and lentils have fairly neutral flavours, but their chewy texture adds layers to the feathery mushrooms. Top it all off with oozing yolks from the best eggs you can get your hands on.*

½ cup beluga lentils, rinsed

½ cup wild black rice, rinsed

2 tablespoons extra virgin olive oil, divided

2 cups Cipollini onions, peeled and halved

Flaky sea salt and freshly cracked black pepper, to season

3 cloves garlic, minced

1 pound (450 grams) maitake mushrooms, woody stems removed (see Note)

2 teaspoons balsamic vinegar

4 eggs

½ cup living sprouts, for garnish (optional)

Good-quality extra virgin olive oil, for serving

In a medium pot with a lid on, bring 2 cups (500 mL) salted water to a boil. Remove the lid, reduce the heat to medium, and add the lentils and rice. Simmer until the lentils and rice are soft, 20 to 25 minutes. Add a little more water during the cooking process if the lentils begin to stick to the bottom of the pan. Once the lentils and rice are fully cooked, drain in a colander to remove any excess liquid. Set aside in a large mixing bowl.

Heat a large skillet over medium. Add 1 tablespoon olive oil and the Cipollini onions. Stir the onions occasionally while they sauté to a blond caramelization, about 8 minutes. Reduce the heat to low, continue to stir every so often, and allow the onions to release more juices for another 5 to 10 minutes. Remove the onions from the heat and add to the mixing bowl with the lentils and rice. Mix everything together once again. Taste and season with salt and pepper as needed.

Reheat the skillet over medium. Add the remaining 1 tablespoon of olive oil and the garlic. Stir until fragrant, 2 to 3 minutes. Reduce the heat to medium-low and add the mushrooms. Sauté for 8 to 10 minutes or until the mushrooms have wilted. Slowly drizzle with the balsamic vinegar and cook on low for 2 minutes, stirring to stop the vinegar from burning. Remove from the heat, lightly salt the mushrooms, and set aside for serving.

recipe continues

To poach the eggs, fill a small pot three-quarters full with water and bring to a boil. Once boiling, swirl the water with a spoon and use the spoon to gently slip the cracked eggs, one at a time, into the water. Start at 12 o'clock and make your way around (this will help you remember which egg to remove first). Turn off the heat, cover the pot with a lid, and let the eggs cook for 3 minutes for soft-poached. Starting at 12 o'clock, use a slotted spoon to remove each egg and place on a paper towel– or tea towel–lined plate to absorb access water before plating.

Divide the lentil rice mixture between four plates. Place the mushrooms over the lentils and rice. Top each dish with a poached egg and garnish with sprouts. Drizzle with a good-quality olive oil and season with salt and pepper before serving.

NOTE: *The unique flavours of maitake mushrooms make them hard to substitute in this recipe, but if you are having a tough time sourcing them, the next best option would be a mix of pioppini and shiitake.*

Sunchoke, Cauliflower & Leek Soup with Canadian Gremolata
Serves 4 to 6

If you are new to the sunchoke (also called a Jerusalem artichoke), you are in for a tender, slightly nutty treat. Sunchokes—very much like potatoes—are hardy tubers, fit for Ontario's cool climate, and they grow wild here throughout the fall and are available all winter. Simmering sunchokes with cauliflower in a pot over low heat allows for the vegetables to steam in their own liquid and turn into a silky cream not unlike a culinary version of cashmere. This zesty gremolata is a Canadian interpretation of a traditional Milanese spice mix. Instead of lemon, I used sumac—a berry with bright red cones that grows wild across Ontario. It can be harvested, dried, and blitzed into a wonderful spice on its own.

Sunchoke, Cauliflower & Leek Soup

1 cup chopped leeks (about 1 stalk, end trimmed and dark green tops removed)

1 tablespoon unsalted butter

2 cloves garlic, minced

2 cups peeled and cubed sunchokes (1½-inch/4 cm cubes), placed in a bowl of cold water

2 cups chopped cauliflower florets

Kosher salt, to season

4 cups (1 litre) vegetable broth

2 bay leaves

1 tablespoon fresh flat-leaf parsley leaves

Freshly cracked black pepper, to season

Canadian Gremolata

1 tablespoon raw, unsalted sunflower seeds

1 teaspoon ground sumac

1 teaspoon fresh thyme leaves

½ teaspoon flaky sea salt

2 cloves garlic, minced

1 cup roughly chopped fresh flat-leaf parsley leaves

Place the chopped leeks in a colander and wash thoroughly. Use your hands to inspect the leeks to ensure the dirt between the layers has been removed. Dry and set aside.

In a large pot over medium, melt the butter. Add the leeks and sauté until caramelized and translucent, about 10 minutes. Use a wooden spoon to stir often. Reduce the heat to medium-low and add the garlic. Stirring frequently, cook until fragrant, 2 to 3 minutes. Remove the sunchokes from the cold-water bath and add them and the cauliflower to the leeks and garlic. Season with salt. Stir and cook for another 2 to 3 minutes. Add the broth and increase the heat to high. Cover with a lid. Once the liquid reaches a boil, reduce the heat to a simmer. Add the bay leaves and parsley and let simmer until the vegetables are fork-tender, about 35 minutes.

While the soup is simmering, in a mortar, grind the sunflower seeds, sumac, thyme, and sea salt with a pestle. Add the garlic and continue to grind until a crunchy paste forms. Add the parsley and continue to stamp, press, and muddle into a minced paste. Set aside for serving.

Remove the pot from the heat, take out the bay leaves, and set the soup aside to cool for 5 to 10 minutes before blending. Use an immersion blender or transfer the soup to a good-quality blender to purée into a thick, creamy soup. Season with salt and pepper to taste. Garnish with 1 to 2 tablespoons of the gremolata, and serve.

Shaved Brussels Sprout Salad with Crispy Sprouts

Serves 8

Like cabbage and kale, Brussels sprouts are descendants of the mustard plant—all hardy and pungent when untreated, but when shavings of Brussels sprouts swim honourably in a decent glug of oil, they crisp up and mellow into addictive vessels for toasted pine nuts and briny capers. A warm fall salad, like this one, is the exact rebranding a Brussels sprout deserves.

---

6 cups Brussels sprouts, divided

6 tablespoons extra virgin olive oil, divided

Kosher salt, to season

¼ cup pine nuts

Juice of 1 lemon

2 tablespoons capers

Freshly cracked black pepper, to season

¼ cup (0.9 ounce/25 grams) freshly shaved Parmesan

1 teaspoon dried chili flakes (optional)

NOTE: *The fastest, easiest way to shave the sprouts is with a food processor fitted with a thin slicing disk (⅛ inch/3 mm or thinner). Alternatively, you can slice them thinly by hand using a chef's knife.*

Preheat the oven to 350°F (175°C) and line a baking sheet with parchment paper. Trim and quarter 2 cups of the Brussels sprouts. Finely shave the remaining 4 cups of Brussels sprouts (see Note).

In a large mixing bowl, combine the quartered Brussels sprouts, 1 tablespoon olive oil, and a generous seasoning of salt. Toss until the quartered sprouts are well coated. Spread them evenly on the prepared baking sheet. Roast for 15 minutes, then take the baking sheet out of the oven and give the sprouts a good toss. This will give both sides of the sprouts a chance to crisp up with golden edges. Place the baking sheet back in the oven for 10 minutes more, or until everything is lightly crisped. Add the pine nuts to the roasting sprouts and cook for another 5 minutes. Set aside the sprouts and pine nuts to cool for just a few minutes.

In the same large mixing bowl used for the quartered sprouts, toss the shaved Brussels sprouts with a generous seasoning of salt. Let stand for 15 minutes. Mix in the lemon juice and the remaining 5 tablespoons olive oil. Use your hands to get messy and massage the sprouts. Once the sprouts are fully coated with the oil, they will have slightly softened. Add in the capers and lightly season with pepper. Again, mix with your hands until everything is well combined. Add the Parmesan and chili flakes. Use salad tossers to lightly mix the ingredients.

Taste the salad and add more salt if needed. Top the salad with crispy sprouts to serve.

Roasted Delicata Squash with Sage Salsa Verde
Serves 4

Delicata squash is one of the only squashes that does not keep throughout the entire winter and is truly best eaten in the fall. Some may say this makes it extra special. The squash can be cut into beautiful rings that look like elegant flowers and can be presented as such on the dinner table. The delicata's sweet flesh is light and surprisingly happy when paired with a sauce made of toasted sage leaves—an ideal sweet-savoury balance.

Sage Salsa Verde

2 tablespoons extra virgin olive oil

¼ cup fresh sage leaves

½ teaspoon flaky sea salt

½ cup finely chopped fresh cilantro leaves

¼ cup finely diced shallots (about 1 shallot)

2 tablespoons sherry vinegar

Delicata Squash

2 large delicata squashes (each about 1½ pounds/680 grams) (see Note)

2 tablespoons extra virgin olive oil

Fine sea salt and freshly cracked black pepper

NOTE: *There's no need to peel the skin on a delicata squash. Delicata gets its name from its delicate, edible rind when cooked.*

In a small skillet over medium-high, heat the olive oil. Once the oil begins to sizzle, add the sage leaves. Cook until the sage leaves crisp up, 2 to 3 minutes. Keep a watchful eye on the sage because it can burn easily and become bitter, so stir often to avoid this. Once cooked, transfer the sage leaves into a mortar. Add the salt and begin to stamp the leaves with the pestle to form a crumbly texture. Add the cilantro, shallots, and vinegar and muddle until everything is well combined. Taste and season with more salt as needed. Set aside for serving.

Preheat the oven to 350°F (175°C) and line a baking sheet with parchment paper.

Cut the squashes in half crosswise (along the equator). This will reserve the squashes' beautiful flower-like shape. Use a spoon to scoop out all the seeds and pith from the squash halves. Use a sharp chef's knife to cut the squashes into ½-inch (1 cm) round flower-shaped slices.

In a medium mixing bowl, toss the squash with the oil, salt, and pepper. Evenly distribute the squash on the prepared baking sheet. To roast the squash evenly, avoid overcrowding the sheet (use two lined baking sheets if necessary). Roast for 35 to 40 minutes, flipping the squash midway through, until browned and soft on the inside. Set aside to cool for a few minutes.

Plate the squash, garnish with the salsa verde, and serve.

Smoky Trout with Horseradish Vinaigrette
Serves 2

Lake trout is found all across Ontario; the name is actually an all-encompassing one for many cold-water species, including rainbow, steelhead, and tiger. All of these are mild fish that pick up the flavours they are cooked in, and if you are like me—with an affinity for smoky flavours—all the better to make this recipe. As the saying goes, opposites attract— pairing this delicate, flaky fish with fall's harvest of pungent horseradish makes for a nice contrast for your taste buds.

Horseradish Vinaigrette

1-inch knob of fresh horseradish

2 tablespoons water

Pinch of kosher salt

2½ tablespoons white wine vinegar

1 tablespoon whole grain mustard

2 tablespoons good-quality extra virgin olive oil

¼ cup coarsely chopped fresh flat-leaf parsley

Smoky Trout

½ pound (225 grams) steelhead trout fillets

¼ cup brown sugar

1 teaspoon fine sea salt

NOTES

Smoking trout without a smoker may sound difficult, but so long as you have a wok, a bamboo steamer, some foil, and hickory chips, you are set.

Smoking fish takes little time, so I suggest preparing your vinaigrette ahead of time.

Use a vegetable peeler to peel the surface skin off the horseradish. Chop into pieces and place in a food processor. Pulse the food processor to get a rough chop. Add the water and salt. Process until well ground. Add the vinegar, mustard, and oil. Pulse to combine. Add the parsley and give the processor three to five pulses. Taste and season with more salt, if needed. Set aside for serving. Extra vinaigrette can be stored in a sealed jar in the refrigerator for up to 1 week.

As if it were a puppy's belly, give the trout a good rub with the brown sugar and salt. Set aside until the smoker is ready.

Line the inside of a wok with two long sheets of foil (about 2 to 3 feet/60 to 90 cm) in a cross shape. The foil will extend beyond the wok like wings and eventually be folded back over everything. Fill the foiled wok with a handful of hickory chips (see Glossary on page 266). Place a 10-inch (25 cm) bamboo steamer on top of the smoking chips. Place the trout in the steamer. Cover the steamer with its lid and wrap with the extended foil wings from the wok. Add more foil if the entire lid is not covered. This will lock in the smoke and help cook everything evenly. Heat the wok on the stove over medium-high for 2 to 3 minutes. Reduce to low and allow the trout to smoke for another 10 minutes. Remove the wok from the heat and let it sit, covered, for 5 minutes to continue to infuse the trout. Unpeel the foil lock, take off the steamer lid, and enjoy your delicious smoked trout with the horseradish vinaigrette. Smoked trout is at its best immediately after smoking but can be enjoyed the next day cold in a salad or on toast.

Tomato Cranberry Chutney

Makes ¾ cup (180 mL)

I developed this chutney recipe for a seasonal meal at Fresh City Farms. We wanted to build a festive, ready-made meal that sang the praises of fall's most celebrated flavours—including turkey, sweet potatoes, and, of course, cranberries. It was available only once a year, but I, like many others, would have thoroughly enjoyed having this chutney on everything, anytime. Sweet and savoury, this thick, jammy sauce can be spread across toast in the morning, added to a charcuterie board, or served on a decadent dinner table with turkey and roasted vegetables. We had requests for this sauce year-round, so I am delighted to share it here for you to enjoy in your home at any time.

2 tablespoons good-quality extra virgin olive oil

1 yellow onion, roughly chopped

2 cloves garlic, minced

½ teaspoon kosher salt

1 large field tomato, seeds removed and diced

½ cup fresh cranberries

2 tablespoons honey

In a large skillet over medium, heat the oil. Once the skillet is hot, sauté the onions to a blond caramelization, about 10 minutes. Reduce the heat to medium-low and add the garlic and salt. Stir and cook until fragrant, 2 to 3 minutes. Add the diced tomatoes and cranberries. Simmer on low for 20 minutes, until the tomatoes and cranberries take on a deep red, jammy consistency. Remove from the heat to cool slightly.

Add the tomato-cranberry mixture and honey to a food processor. Pulse until everything is well incorporated but still slightly chunky. Taste and season with more salt, if needed. If you are not using your chutney right away, that's a moment of delight missed, but I am excited for your future self because this chutney can be stored in a sealed container in the refrigerator for up to 2 weeks, and it pairs well with more than just turkey.

The Leftovers Sandwich

Serves 2

The sandwich to end all sandwiches! A smorgasbord of leftovers, sandwiched between two slices of fresh sourdough, toasted just enough to withhold the weight of the jammy, sweet-and-savoury cranberry chutney, and the onion-garlic-turkey-bacon sauté (scents so enticing it will summon an entire household of sleepy-heads) is quite possibly the greatest sandwich one can experience. Top it with a fresh crunch of lettuce and a fried egg with a runny yolk that dribbles out, enough to make you lean over your plate. What was neglected the night before has now been transformed into a masterpiece.

---

2 slices bacon

1 yellow onion, sliced

1 tablespoon extra virgin olive oil, plus an extra tablespoon if needed when cooking onions

2 cloves garlic, minced

6 ounces (170 grams) leftover turkey (both dark and white), pulled

Kosher salt and freshly cracked black pepper

2 eggs

¼ cup (60 mL) Tomato Cranberry Chutney (page 176)

4 slices fresh sourdough, toasted

2 leaves leaf lettuce

Heat a skillet over medium and add the bacon slices. Cook to ideal crispness (6 to 8 minutes, flipping midway), then transfer the bacon to a paper towel–lined plate, keeping the bacon fat in the pan.

Add the onions to the skillet with the bacon fat and turn the heat to medium-low. Stirring regularly, cook the onions until golden, about 10 minutes. Add 1 tablespoon oil if the onions begin to stick. Add the garlic and stir with a wooden spoon until fragrant, about 2 to 3 minutes. Add the turkey and sauté until the turkey warms up, 2 to 3 minutes. Transfer the turkey fry to a medium mixing bowl and crumble the bacon in. Season with salt and pepper. Mix everything into a well-combined hash.

Clean and dry the skillet. With the skillet over medium, heat 1 tablespoon oil. Once the oil begins to sizzle, crack the eggs into the pan and fry until the whites are opaque, edges are browned, and yolks are cooked to your desired doneness. Remove from the heat and set aside to assemble the sandwiches.

Spread 2 tablespoons chutney onto each of two slices of sourdough toast. Place the lettuce leaves on top of the chutney. Top with the fried eggs and the turkey-bacon hash. Top both sandwiches with the remaining pieces of toast. Cut in half and serve.

Plum Port Tart

Makes one 9-inch (23 cm) tart

This tart will be different from batch to batch, depending on the 40-plus plum options available to you in Ontario. If you happen to find the Satsuma plum (the sweet honey and wine plum I grew up picking in my Baba and Didi's home in the suburbs of Toronto), you are doubly blessed. All options are delicious, and here they're sweetly intensified by a port anise reduction that floods the pastry. As soon as you put the tart in the oven, you will be punch-drunk from the fruity aromas of the plums simmering in their own juices and spices. Serve warm with a dollop of cream, or relaxed at room temperature.

Forgiving Flaky Tart Crust

1¼ cups (150 grams) all-purpose flour (or gluten-free flour blend; see Note, page 148)

½ cup (100 grams) granulated sugar

½ teaspoon fine sea salt

½ cup (120 grams) cold unsalted butter, cut into ½-inch (1 cm) cubes

1 teaspoon pure vanilla extract

Plum Port Filling

2 cups (500 mL) port wine

½ cup (105 grams) brown sugar, plus 1 tablespoon for sprinkling

¼ teaspoon anise seeds, crushed

1½ pounds (680 grams) plums (5 to 6 medium), pitted and quartered

1 tablespoon all-purpose flour (or gluten-free flour blend; see Note, page 148)

Make the Forgiving Flaky Tart Crust: Preheat the oven to 350°F (175°C). Lightly butter a 9-inch (23 cm) tart pan.

In a food processor (see Note), place the flour, sugar, and salt and process until combined, about 5 seconds. Add the butter and vanilla to the food processor and pulse until it has a coarse but evenly moist sand texture, about 12 to 14 pulses. Crumble the dough into the prepared tart pan and press into an even layer over the bottom and up the sides. Prick the surface of the dough a few times with a fork and place in the freezer for 15 minutes to chill.

Bake the tart crust until golden brown, about 15 minutes. Transfer the tart pan to a wire rack and let it cool completely before adding the plums. Keep the oven on and increase the temperature to 375°F (190°C).

Make the Plum Port Filling: In a large skillet over high heat, bring the port to a boil. Add ½ cup (105 grams) brown sugar and the anise seeds. With a spoon, continuously swirl the port in a circle until it has reduced to ⅔ cup (160 mL) of thick-as-honey syrup. This will take about 15 minutes. Any shorter and you will likely end up with a thin syrup and a soggy bottom.

Place the plums into a large mixing bowl. Sprinkle the flour over the plums and toss to coat. Drizzle the thick port syrup over the plums and toss again until the plums are nice and sticky. Arrange the gooey coated plums evenly in the cooled, baked tart crust. If there is remaining syrup in the bowl, now is your chance to drizzle it over the plums.

Bake the Tart: Bake the tart until the juices are bubbling, the fruit is tender, and the crust is golden, 30 to 35 minutes. Transfer to a wire rack to cool and allow the filling to set for 10 minutes, then remove the tart from the tart pan (if you decide to remove the tart—serving in the tart pan works just as well). Plum port tarts are equally delicious the next day. Store in an airtight container or tightly wrapped in plastic wrap in the refrigerator for up to 4 days.

Coronation Grape Schiacciata

Serves 10

Schiacciata is essentially a fruit focaccia and is traditionally made with grapes in Tuscany, where it hails from (also known as schiacciata all'uva). It's a fluffy dough baked to a golden crisp and stained by the bursts of purple Coronation grapes. The more stains, the better, and that is why I will always stray from the traditional Tuscan recipe and double up on the grapes. I make it a 2:1 grape-to-dough ratio.

½ tablespoon (4 grams) instant dry yeast

1 tablespoon + ½ cup (125 mL) lukewarm water, divided

1 tablespoon + ¼ cup (25 grams) granulated sugar, divided

2½ cups (310 grams) all-purpose flour

Good-quality extra virgin olive oil, for coating and drizzling

2 cups Coronation grapes (or blueberries) (see Note)

NOTE: *These sweet-on-the-inside, tart-on-the-outside grapes grow rapidly around Lake Ontario at this time of year and are really only available until the end of October.*

In a small mixing bowl, mix the yeast with 1 tablespoon lukewarm water and 1 tablespoon sugar. Set aside for 10 minutes, until bubbles begin to form. This will confirm the yeast is alive.

Sift the flour into a large mixing bowl. Mix in the active yeast mixture. Slowly begin to pour the remaining ½ cup (125 mL) water into the mixing bowl and combine everything together with your hands. Continue to mix until the flour absorbs all the water and a ball of dough forms. If the dough has a batter-like consistency, stop and adjust with more flour. Knead the dough on a well-floured surface until a silky-smooth consistency is formed, about 6 minutes.

Coat a mixing bowl with oil and place the dough into the bowl. Cover the bowl with a damp tea towel and set in a cool, dry area until the dough rises and doubles in size, at least 1 hour.

Preheat the oven to 350°F (175°C) and line a 9- × 13-inch (23 × 33 cm) baking sheet with parchment paper. On a well-floured surface, roll out the dough into a rectangular shape, ¼ inch (0.5 cm) thick. Gently stretch the dough to the edge of the prepared baking sheet by placing your hands underneath and pulling outward. Push down all corners and sides. With wet fingers, push down to make craters all over the schiacciata. Scatter the grapes over top. Sprinkle the remaining ¼ cup (25 grams) sugar on top of the grapes and drizzle with oil.

Bake until the schiacciata is golden on top and appears golden on the underside (lift a corner of the schiacciata—careful not to burn your fingers—and take a peek), 20 to 25 minutes. After baking, set aside to cool just enough to handle, about 15 minutes. Cut into squares and serve. Schiacciata is at its best the day of baking but will keep at room temperature in an airtight container for another day.

How To: Quick Pickle Vegetables

Makes two 16-ounce (473 mL) jars (4 cups/1 litre total)

I would love to say that I always compose impromptu dishes from vegetables I just picked up at the market. This does happen sometimes, but more often, repurposing leftovers or an array of odds and ends makes for an excellent throw-together meal, especially when brightened by a slightly sweet, tangy pickled vegetable.

So the question of what to pickle at this time of the year? Burdock is fun because it is a rarely used, in-season root that will shock and awe, not only yourself but those you are serving. Burdock is slender and brown and looks like a stack of sticks. However, when you uncover what is underneath the skin, there is an ivory, parsnip-like, earthy, semisweet root. Or maybe try turnip: the large round roots look like radish's big uncle and taste like a potato and a carrot mated. Another good one to have at the ready is the crisp radish. Both a warm- and cold-weather crop, there are many varieties to choose from, ranging on the pungency scale from mild (daikon) to very pungent (black radish). When pickled, even the most bitter or pungent vegetables sweeten under the spell of a salt-water-acid brine.

Equipment

2 clean jars with sealable snap lids (each 16 ounces/473 mL)

1 medium saucepan

Quick Pickled Vegetables

2 cups vegetables (mixed or solo)

· Burdock, peeled and thinly sliced

· Onions (red, shallots), peeled and thinly sliced

· Radishes (black, Easter egg, red, daikon), thinly sliced

· Turnips, peeled and thinly sliced

· Carrots, peeled and sliced into ribbons using a vegetable peeler

· Cauliflower, chopped into bite-size florets

1 teaspoon mustard seeds

1 teaspoon coriander seeds

1 cup (250 mL) water

1 cup (250 mL) apple cider vinegar

3 cloves garlic, smashed

1 tablespoon kosher salt

Divide your chosen vegetables into the two jars, packing the vegetables tightly. Ensure there is 1 inch (2.5 cm) of space at the top of each jar. Divide the mustard and coriander seeds equally between the jars.

Add the water, vinegar, garlic, and salt to a medium saucepan over high heat. Once the liquid reaches a boil, remove the saucepan from the heat, stir to mix everything well, and pour the brine over the vegetables. Fill the jars, still making sure to leave a 1 inch (2.5 cm) space at the top. Gently tap the jars on the counter to remove any air bubbles. Tightly seal the jars with their lids. Flip the jars upside down and back to right side up (the heat from the liquid will prevent the potential growth of bacteria). Let the jars cool to room temperature.

Store the quick pickled vegetables in the refrigerator. The pickles will improve in flavour over time. Try to wait at least 48 hours before cracking them open, but they can be used as soon as 1 hour after preparation. These pickled vegetables will last in the refrigerator for up to 2 weeks.

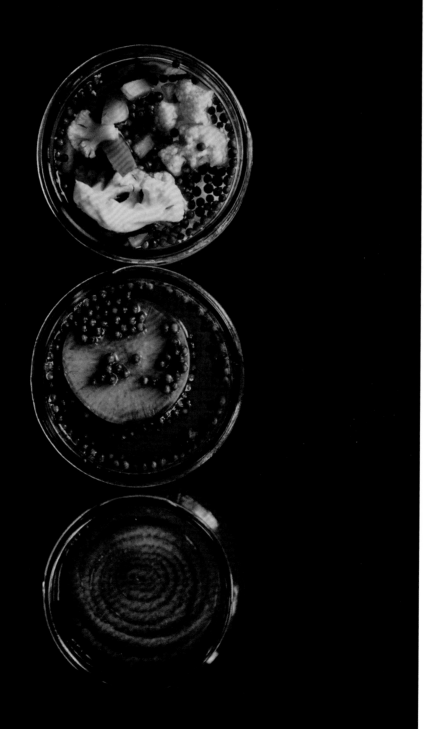

Sumac Crème Fraîche, Lox & Pickled Radish with Montreal-Style Bagels
Serves 2 to 4

I have a profound fondness for a good bagel and lox display. Most Sunday mornings, there would be a colourful parade of accoutrements passed around the table in my childhood home. To keep that allure, I've kept things classic but threw a little peak-season twist into the mix here. Lemon was switched over to sumac—an electric red flower native to Ontario. In the late fall, their exotic appearance sticks out like a sore thumb all across snowy-white northern country roads. Every May (after all the rain and before the bugs get in there), I harvest clusters of sumac (called bobs), dry out their velvety berries over the summer, and blitz them into spice by fall. Today, sumac is a common spice in Middle Eastern cooking, but I don't see any good reason why sumac shouldn't be sitting in a shaker on every kitchen table in Ontario. It is a great substitute for citrus and an even better seasoning to mix into a crème fraîche and spread on a bagel. And without getting into too much of a debate, Montreal bagels are the best for this type of dish. They are cooked in a wood-fired oven, which give them a chewier, richer crust. Enjoy them warm in fine company with said Sumac Crème Fraîche, buttery lox, a few pickled radishes, and pickled onions.

Sumac Crème Fraîche

½ cup (125 mL) crème fraîche (or cream cheese)

1 teaspoon ground sumac

1 teaspoon white wine vinegar

Kosher salt, to season

To Serve

2 Montreal-style bagels, cut in half

¼ cup quick pickled radishes (page 184)

½ pound (225 grams) smoked salmon

2 tablespoons quick pickled onions (page 184)

1½ tablespoons capers

Good-quality extra virgin olive oil, for drizzling

1 handful fresh dill, roughly torn

Freshly cracked black pepper, to season

In a small mixing bowl, whisk the crème fraîche, sumac, vinegar, and salt together until well combined. Taste and season with more salt, if needed. Set aside for spreading and reserve any extra in a sealed container (I like to repurpose the crème fraîche container here) for up to 3 days.

Spread the sumac crème fraîche evenly across each bagel slice. Place four to six slices of pickled radish on each bagel and layer on the smoked salmon. Top with pickled onions and capers. Drizzle the bagels with olive oil. Sprinkle with dill and season with pepper to serve.

Golden Pear & Pickled Roots Salad

Serves 4

This isn't just a regular old salad. It's a fall salad with a mix of distinct flavours: sweet, bitter, acidic, salty, and umami (the fifth sense of taste). A sweet-nutty pear is the in-season feature—I like to use Bosc or another firm pear that retains its crunchy texture when cooked. Then there's the vibrant pickled radishes that are even more convenient if you already have them in your refrigerator waiting to be used (see page 184). And praise be to bitter hardy greens, like mustard greens—nature's way of providing us with phytonutrients and keeping us healthy in the colder months. In addition to the array of flavours on display here, this salad is really easy to whip together. The only real effort comes from emulsifying the vinaigrette in a blender. Some people shy away from anchovies, but they are discrete enough here. You won't notice a fishy flavour; rather, they provide the deeply satiating umami element to the vinaigrette. There's nothing overpowering going on, but the vinaigrette lifts up and brings together each character in this interesting yet relaxed salad.

Anchovy Vinaigrette

¼ cup (60 mL) good-quality extra virgin olive oil

1½ tablespoons red wine vinegar

2 anchovy fillets (including 1 to 2 tablespoons residual oil)

1 tablespoon grainy mustard

½ shallot, roughly chopped

2 tablespoons water

Kosher salt and freshly cracked black pepper

Golden Pear & Pickled Roots Salad

1 pear, cored and thinly sliced

2 cups mustard greens (or arugula, spinach, or a mixture), roughly torn into bite-size pieces

¾ cup quick pickled radishes and/or burdock (see page 184)

2 teaspoons coriander seeds

¼ cup (0.9 ounce/25 grams) freshly shaved Parmesan

In a blender, blend the oil, vinegar, anchovies, and mustard for 1 minute. Add the shallots and pulse a few times until minced. Slowly pour in the water and continue to blend until everything has emulsified. Season with salt and pepper. Set aside.

Preheat the oven to 400°F (200°C) and line a baking sheet with parchment paper. Evenly spread the sliced pears on the prepared baking sheet without overcrowding. Place the baking sheet on the bottom rack of the oven and roast until the pears are golden on the outside but soft on the inside, about 15 minutes. Set aside to cool.

Plate the greens and cooked pears evenly among four plates. Top with the pickled radishes and/or burdock and the coriander seeds. Drizzle the salad with the anchovy vinaigrette and garnish with the Parmesan to serve.

Roasted Carrots & Burrata with Carrot-Top Chimichurri

Serves 4

This showstopper of a dish proficiently uses the entire anatomy of a carrot, from top to bottom. In November, you'll notice that carrots still have vibrant green fronds on their heads, locks that look similar to fresh dill but have more of a mild parsley taste to them. When prepared alongside a few other aromatics, they make for a delicious chimichurri—an Argentinian sauce with a fresh herbaceous flavour that illuminates an already sweet set of rainbow carrots. The carrots are tossed in olive oil, garlic, and salt, then roasted on high heat until the insides are tender but the edges are golden crisp. This is how I declare all carrots should be enjoyed—in peak season, dressed in chimichurri, and with a ball of velvety burrata on top.

Carrot-Top Chimichurri

(makes 1 cup/250 mL)

½ cup reserved carrot-top greens

1 cup roughly chopped cilantro

2 cloves garlic

1 tablespoon dried oregano

1½ tablespoons red wine vinegar

¾ cup (180 mL) extra virgin olive oil

1 teaspoon kosher salt

Roasted Carrots

2 tablespoons good-quality extra virgin olive oil

1 pound (450 grams) carrots with green tops, scrubbed (tops reserved for chimichurri and garnish)

3 cloves garlic, crushed

1 teaspoon kosher salt

To Finish

1 ball (8.8 ounces/250 grams) fresh burrata

2 tablespoons raw unsalted pumpkin seeds

In the small bowl of a food processor, combine the carrot-top greens, cilantro, garlic, oregano, and vinegar. Pulse until everything is coarsely ground. Slowly add the olive oil and pulse into a chunky paste. Season with salt, taste, and adjust as needed. Set aside for serving. Any extra chimichurri can be stored, sealed in a jar or airtight container, in the refrigerator for up to 4 days.

Preheat the oven to 400°F (200°C). In a large oven-safe skillet over medium-high, heat the oil. Add the carrots and cook, rotating once or twice, until browned on all sides, about 8 minutes. Add the garlic and continue to cook until fragrant, 2 to 3 minutes. Season the garlicky carrots with salt and place the oven-safe skillet into the oven to roast. Cook until the carrots are soft but with enough bite that they stay firm when lifted, about 20 minutes. Set aside to cool for 5 minutes before plating.

Plate the carrots and drizzle ⅓ cup (80 mL) of the chimichurri over top. Nestle the burrata onto the bed of carrots. Sprinkle the pumpkin seeds and remaining carrot-top greens over top. Serve the extra chimichurri on the side.

Bison Flank Steak with Carrot-Top Chimichurri

Serves 4

Bison is the buffalo of Canada. To cook bison is to enjoy a special meal with not much fuss but plenty of reverence. Once threatened with extinction and now recovered, bison are precious creatures. And that is good, because herein sits a reminder that food is something to be appreciated and cooked with care. Cuts like flank need only 8 minutes of cooking time over high heat, and when you slice into their cherry-pink centres, the meat will almost melt in your mouth. This meat is not gamey, but rather tender, juicy, and full of flavour—less greasy than beef and just a bit sweeter. I love serving this with a vibrant, punchy sauce like Carrot-Top Chimichurri (page 191), which complements and brings out the flank's slightly sweet flavours.

½ cup (125 mL) + 1 tablespoon grapeseed oil, divided

¼ cup (60 mL) balsamic vinegar

1 tablespoon honey

2 teaspoons juniper berries, crushed

1 teaspoon kosher salt

1 teaspoon dried chili flakes (optional)

4 cloves garlic, minced

2 pounds (900 grams) bison flank steak (see Note)

½ cup (125 mL) Carrot-Top Chimichurri (page 191)

In a small bowl, combine the ½ cup (125 mL) oil, balsamic vinegar, honey, juniper berries, salt, chili flakes, and garlic. Whisk until everything is well mixed. Place the steaks in a deep dish and pour the marinade over the steaks. Cover the dish and refrigerate for 1 hour or up to 24 hours.

In a large skillet over medium-high, heat the remaining 1 tablespoon oil. Once the oil is sizzling, shake off excess marinade before placing the meat in the hot skillet to cook. Cook the steaks, 4 to 5 minutes per side, or until an instant-read thermometer inserted into the centre of the steak reaches 135°F (57°C) (for medium-rare). If your skillet does not fit all the steaks with 1 inch (2.5 cm) of space between them, cook in batches so as not to overcrowd the pan. Let the steaks rest for 4 minutes before slicing. Slice against the grain and serve with the carrot-top chimichurri.

NOTE: *You can find different cuts of bison at most local butchers, but beef flank steak works as a good substitute.*

Romanesco Broccoli Cacio e Pepe

Serves 4

This is a meal made for a frosty November evening dining in, or even better, a date night—when the pinnacle of the brassicas are in peak season and a bowl of cacio e pepe can comfort and satiate. I like to use the supple bucatini noodle, a thicker version of spaghetti with a central hole through the centre to absorb and escort its creamy peppery sauce. And if I were to nominate any vegetable to chastely accompany Pecorino- and pepper-laden noodles, it would be the brilliantly geometric Romanesco broccoli. Built like a castle, the florets here are seasoned and roasted until fork-tender and the edges are caramel gold. It is a simple thing, really, to cook pasta to al dente and mix it with a few thoughtfully chosen ingredients— creamy cheese, spiky pepper, and a flash of brilliant green Romanesco broccoli. Your meal is ready as soon as you light the candles and pour the wine.

2 cups Romanesco broccoli florets (1 head; see Note)

Kosher salt, to season

2 tablespoons olive oil

1 cup (3½ ounces/100 grams) freshly grated Pecorino

1 cup (3½ ounces/100 grams) freshly grated Parmesan, plus more for serving

2 teaspoons freshly cracked black pepper

12 ounces (340 grams) fresh bucatini pasta (or tagliolini or spaghetti)

NOTE: *Upon first glance, you may not recognize the Romanesco broccoli because it is not as ubiquitous in supermarkets as its siblings, broccoli and cauliflower. In November, it can be found at most markets and grocers that specialize in local produce.*

Preheat the oven to 400°F (200°C) and line a baking sheet with parchment paper.

In a large mixing bowl, coat the Romanesco florets with a generous seasoning of salt and the oil. Spread the florets on the baking sheet and roast until fork-tender and golden brown, about 20 minutes.

Meanwhile, in a large bowl, combine the Pecorino, Parmesan, and black pepper and patiently wait to lay the pasta on top.

In a large pot over high, heat 8 cups (2 litres) water seasoned generously with salt. Once the water begins to boil, reduce the heat to medium and add the pasta. Cook the pasta until al dente, 3 minutes. Strain the pasta, reserving ¼ cup (60 mL) of the pasta water for the sauce. Add the pasta to the mixing bowl with the cheese and pepper. Use two large forks to mix the pasta with the cheese and pepper until well combined. Pour in the reserved pasta water and continue to mix until a creamy sauce coats every noodle.

Divide the pasta among four shallow bowls. Divide the roasted Romanesco among the four bowls. Season with salt and pepper as necessary. Garnish with a little extra Parmesan and serve.

Kimchi Cauliflower Bibimbap

Serves 2

Every time I eat a bowl of bibimbap, I think about how this magical mélange of ingredients comes together perfectly every time. But that is the beauty of Korean cooking—it's all about layers of flavour and is extensively customizable. As a means of celebrating this month's peak-season ingredients, I've used cauliflower as a substitute for the traditional rice in this dish, and layered in ingredients of flattery: kimchi, which provides all the umami funk to the dish, spicy-sweet gochujang, salty kelp flakes, crunchy seeds, and a fresh kick of green onions. Such a sensorial dish can be topped with a crispy-edged fried egg—best to let the canary-yellow yolk seep out and mix in with its bowl mates.

1 small head cauliflower, stem and leaves removed (about 2 cups/500 mL florets)

2 tablespoons sunflower oil, divided

1 cup roughly chopped kimchi (see Note)

¼ cup (60 mL) kimchi brine

3 tablespoons gochujang (see Note)

2 teaspoons toasted sesame oil

1 clove garlic, minced

¼ cup (60 mL) water, if needed

2 tablespoons tamari

2 eggs

2 green onions, diagonally chopped, for garnish

1 tablespoon kelp flakes, for garnish

1 tablespoon toasted sunflower seeds, for garnish

Break the cauliflower into large florets. Using a food processor with the grater attachment, feed the florets, ¼ cup (60 mL) at a time, into the processor to form a rice-like consistency.

In a large skillet over medium-high, heat 1 tablespoon oil. Add the kimchi and stir-fry for 2 minutes. Add the cauliflower rice, kimchi brine, gochujang, toasted sesame oil, and garlic. Fry for another 5 minutes, or until the cauliflower softens and lightly browns. If the liquid reduces too much and ingredients begin to stick, add the water, 1 tablespoon at a time. Remove the skillet from the heat and mix in the tamari. Divide the kimchi cauliflower rice between two plates and set to the side. Clean the skillet for reuse.

In the same large skillet over medium-high, heat the remaining 1 tablespoon oil. Once the oil is sizzling, fry the eggs until the whites are opaque, edges are browned, and yolks are cooked to your desired doneness.

Top each serving with a fried egg. Garnish with green onions, kelp flakes, and toasted sunflower seeds.

NOTES

I loved learning how to make kimchi from Mama Lee of Kimchi Korea House in Toronto. She makes my favourite kimchi in the city.

Gochujang is a Korean spicy fermented red chili paste. It can be found in Korean grocery stores and most supermarkets.

Baking-Sheet Coq au Vin

Serves 4

There is a dinner I turn to when I can't be bothered to spend a lot of time in the kitchen. It involves switching on the oven, plunking a few ingredients onto a pan, adding a splash of olive oil and wine and a few more aromatics, and slipping the pan into the oven for 45 minutes or so. What emerges is a commingling of golden-crusted chicken thighs, fragrant from the sage and rosemary, in a sea of crispy puffed cannellini beans ready to mop up all the delicious juices. This dish was conceived in my Fresh City Farms test kitchen as a meal kit with busy, hungry city folks in mind. Now I make it all the time and think a more appropriate name for it would be pian e sit (a Hokkien phrase meaning "conveniently cooked"). The dish involves 10 minutes' preparation, if that, and as a result you have a grand meal and the smell of pure, honest cooking. Coq au vin traditionalists will be rolling their eyes at this version, but I hope a sheet-pan meal doesn't stop anyone from making such a wonderful dish.

8 chicken thighs, skin on (about 20 ounces/570 grams)

Kosher salt and freshly cracked black pepper

3 cloves garlic, minced

1 Vidalia onion, cut into wedges

Good-quality extra virgin olive oil, for drizzling

2 cups quartered cremini mushrooms

1 cup cannellini beans, rinsed

2 tablespoons chopped fresh sage (or 1 teaspoon dried)

1 tablespoon fresh rosemary (or ½ teaspoon dried)

¼ cup (60 mL) dry white wine

Fresh loaf of bread, to soak up the flavours (optional)

Preheat the oven to 400°F (200°C).

Rub the chicken thighs with salt, pepper, and garlic. Arrange the chicken thighs and onions evenly across a baking sheet. Drizzle olive oil over the chicken and onions. Roast for 30 minutes.

Remove the baking sheet from the oven and add the mushrooms, beans, sage, rosemary, and wine. Give everything a good stir and roast until the chicken has crispy brown skin and is cooked through (an instant-read thermometer should read 165°F/74°C when inserted into the thickest part of the thigh), about 15 minutes more. Set aside to cool for 5 minutes before serving. A good loaf of fresh bread is always a nice addition to soak up the extra juices here.

Apple Cranberry Pecan Crisp
Serves 6

This marvellously easy crisp is a nice treat to serve and it feels like a warm after-dinner hug. A good crisp recipe can be made any time of year—which fruits I choose depends on what is in peak season. In November, cranberry and apples are top of mind. One of Ontario's native fruits, the scarlet-red cranberry, has a tartness particularly well suited to sweet desserts such as this. When paired with apples, the two soften and bubble together into a cocoon of brown sugar and oats, along with a decadent local nut, the pecan. Serve your crisp warm in its bakeware for your guests to scoop into their allotted bowls, and of course, always, always serve a little ice cream alongside.

Crisp Topping

¾ cup (95 grams) all-purpose flour (or gluten-free flour blend; see Note, page 148)

⅔ cup (65 grams) rolled oats

⅓ cup (70 grams) brown sugar

¼ cup (32 grams) crushed pecans

¼ teaspoon ground cinnamon

¼ teaspoon kosher salt

¾ cup (180 grams) cold unsalted butter, cut into cubes

Apple Cranberry Filling

1 pound (450 grams) apples (about 3 to 4), peeled, cored, and diced to the size of a cranberry

3 cups (300 grams) fresh cranberries

⅔ cup (130 grams) granulated sugar

2 teaspoons ground sumac

1 tablespoon apple cider vinegar

4 teaspoons potato starch (or arrowroot starch)

Vanilla ice cream, for serving (optional)

Preheat the oven to 375°F (190°C).

In a food processor, combine the flour, oats, sugar, pecans, cinnamon, and salt and pulse twice to mix. Add the butter and pulse a few more times, until the mixture forms small crumbles. Alternatively, if you are not feeling up to pulling out the food processor, place the flour, oats, sugar, pecans, cinnamon, and salt in a large bowl and use a large spoon or your hands to mix until well incorporated. Add the butter and continue to mix with your hands until you have formed a crumbly dough. Set aside.

In a large mixing bowl, toss the apples and cranberries with the sugar, sumac, apple cider vinegar, and potato starch. Pour the apple and cranberry mixture into a 9- × 13-inch (23 × 33 cm) baking dish. Sprinkle the crisp topping over the fruit.

Bake the crisp until the fruit is bubbling and the topping is golden, 45 to 50 minutes. Serve warm with a dollop of vanilla ice cream, if desired.

Winter

AS SOON AS THE BITTER STING of a dark winter arrives, many of us huddle into our little dens, waiting for the first tulip buds to appear. It's a rare sighting to catch an Ontarian outdoors in the winter, and if you are so lucky, you will hardly recognize them inside their puffy jackets and balaclavas. But it is on the coldest nights that stars are their brightest and sunchokes are their sweetest.

While the world regenerates in its natural rhythm, the weather forces me to slow down and these months become my favourite time to develop recipes. I spend much more of my time at home, with little to do but explore new ways to make a beet taste just as interesting as it did 3 months prior (Smoked Beet Carpaccio, anyone?). The vegetables that are in season are among my favourites of the year, and many are storage vegetables, harvested before frost but able to last in root cellars for most of the winter. If you live in Ontario, you have a good idea of what some of these vegetables are; they include beets (as noted above), celeriac, turnips, kohlrabi, hardy greens, cabbages, squashes, potatoes, carrots, and parsnips. These vegetables are often warm, earthy, grounding, and full of sustenance when we are stuck in a frigid atmosphere known as the "hunger gap." These are the unsung heroes of the season. If I can convince friends and family members that a whole head of cabbage will make a very exciting dinner, or that a salad can be enjoyed in –4°F (–20°C) weather, I have had a successful winter.

A Winter Wheat Berry Salad (page 238) is a reminder that not all salads have to be dainty. I like to have broth at the ready all winter to keep me warm and help bear the cold snap of February winds. And if there were ever a time and place for dessert, it is in December, in the form of a Pear Custard Tart with Roasted Chestnuts (page 225). It may be piercingly cold, but Ontario is a whimsical place when coated in snow, and hardy kale will still emerge from under the frost.

How To: Build a Great Charcuterie Board

A charcuterie board laden with meats and cheeses is what I imagine as my own personal deli. And like a child given an inch of autonomy, I find it easy to get overwhelmed by the freedom of choices as I try to pick flavours that flatter. The basics for building a balanced charcuterie board are a good thing to know—especially in December, when the snow-dusted streets of Ontario make everyone want to huddle inside for meals together and it becomes a birthright to host a party. Even the most organized hosts have experienced that Tasmanian devil moment at the beginning of a dinner party when everyone seems to show up at the same time but you have yet to put the potatoes in the oven. A legitimate way to keep guests busy is to conjure up a big wooden board adorned with an array of meats, cheeses, fruits, nuts, and preserves and let them serve themselves into a blissful stupor. And if not hosting a crowd but dining as only one or two, there is no more pleasant a supper than a charcuterie board with plenty of good red wine.

I have put together a simple plan to guide you—the rest is up to you and your palate. Your charcuterie board can change shape depending on what meats and cheeses you prefer and what's available to you. Plan for 2 ounces (60 grams) of meat and 2 ounces (60 grams) of cheese per person. That is about four thin slices of meat and two hefty pieces of cheese. Pick the things that are in season (such as a December pear, chestnuts, or a cranberry chutney), find makers that specialize in ingredients you love, and follow this simple template.

Servingware

1 large serving board or cutting board (10 × 20 inches/25 × 51 cm is a good size; I like long and narrow to avoid too much reaching into the centre)

3+ cheese knives (I use antique butter knives; if you can find ones with small handles, you are set)

3+ meat forks or knives (depending on the type of meats you use)

Additional small spoons, forks, or knives for other accoutrements (think jams, pickles, fruits, etc.)

Small plates or serviettes for guests to set their choices

The Basics

To keep things simple, start with the staples. Three cheeses and three meat options to begin. Here are some examples of the variations I like to use. Once you have a charcuterie board filled with the basics, you can begin to add on as you please.

Three cheeses
- 1 soft: Camembert, Riopelle de I'Isle, chèvre
- 1 hard: 3-year-plus Cheddar, aged Gouda, le Fleur des Monts
- 1 adventurous: Bleu Bénédictin, Humboldt Fog, Mimolette

Three meats (if serving meat)
- 1 crudo (cured and sliced): bresaola, 'nduja, cacciatore
- 1 mousse/pâté (delicious terrines made from local ingredients): pâté de campagne, mushroom pâté
- 1 cotto (cooked): prosciutto cotto, roasted bone marrow, chorizo

recipe continues

Two starches
- Something soft: a fresh baguette, sliced
- Something crunchy: water crackers

The Add-Ons

Sour items like **mustard** and **pickled vegetables** will help cut the fat from the meats.

Sweet items like **fresh** or **dried fruits** and **jams** will contrast with saltier foods like salted nuts, pickled items, and salty cheeses and/or meats.

Crunchy items like sliced fennel, pickled radishes, and crudités add dimension while keeping it all fresh.

Pick two or three of these options:
- Walnuts or chestnuts, roasted
- Fresh local honey or preserved apricot jam (from this year's picking)
- Dried pears, apples, or apricots
- Pepper or wine jelly
- Sliced fennel, radishes, endives, or kohlrabi
- Quick pickled vegetables (see page 184)
- Extra-grainy Dijon mustard

NOTES

Make everything finger-friendly or easily spreadable with a knife.

Know your audience and how adventurous they may be with flavours. I like to please my guests' requests with the addition of one or two new items they may never have tried. I reserve the unique blue cheeses, like Bleu Bénédictin, for my extreme-food friends.

Cured meats such as prosciutto are saltier and more intense, so balance them with the fattiness and sweetness of cooked meats like ham.

Apple Celeriac Salad with Pancetta & Pecans

Serves 4

Salads in the winter are usually a hard pass for me. But I will always make an exception, especially when winter ingredients cozy up together in both contrast and balance. In this salad, the sturdy bitter greens are the pacifiers to a "sweet as apple pie" dressing. Toasted pecans and pancetta add a salty crunch, and to shake things up, celeriac—not an entirely popular vegetable to cook with—provides a welcome change from more common sweet roots. Celeriac's linen-white skin is pretty gnarly and filled with craters and divots that do have a certain moonlight charm to them. Peeling isn't as treacherous as the hairy knots imply—a sharp chef's knife will do. What follows is a light, fresh-tasting bite with hints of celery and hazelnut that works well with the tangy slices of crabapples. This is a nice meal on its own, but a more substantial choice is to pair it with seared duck (page 218).

Apple Maple Dressing

¾ cup (180 mL) apple cider vinegar

¼ cup (60 mL) pure maple syrup

1 Gala apple, peeled, cored, and roughly diced

1 clove garlic, minced

1 teaspoon fresh thyme leaves

1 to 2 tablespoons white wine vinegar

Pinch of kosher salt

½ cup (125 mL) grapeseed oil

¼ cup (60 mL) canola oil

Apple Celeriac Salad

5 slices pancetta (or thick-cut bacon)

¾ cup pecans

4 handfuls dandelion greens (or arugula or spinach), chiffonade

¼ celeriac, peeled and thinly sliced (about ½ cup/125 mL) (see Note)

3 crabapples (or Braeburn or Granny Smith apples), cored and thinly sliced into half-moons (see Note)

In a small skillet over medium-low, heat the apple cider vinegar. Add the maple syrup and reduce the heat to low until the liquid thickens and changes to a darker caramel colour, 4 to 6 minutes. Add the apples and garlic. Sauté until the apples are cooked through, stirring every so often, about 7 minutes.

Remove the skillet from the heat and put the apple mixture in a blender along with the thyme, white wine vinegar, and a pinch of salt. Blend for 30 seconds. Slowly add the grapeseed oil and canola oil. Continue to blend until the dressing has fully emulsified. Taste and season with more salt, if desired. Set aside. The dressing can be made up to 4 days ahead and stored in a sealed jar or container in the refrigerator.

Line a plate with paper towel. Heat a large skillet over medium and cook the pancetta until crispy on all sides, 5 to 7 minutes. Transfer the pancetta to the paper towel–lined plate. Wipe down the skillet and place back on the stove over medium heat. Add the pecans to toast, giving them a good stir every so often, about 5 minutes.

In a large mixing bowl, lightly toss the greens with the pancetta, toasted pecans, celeriac, and crabapples. Pour ¼ cup (60 mL) of the dressing over the salad and toss well before serving.

recipe continues

NOTES

To peel celeriac, use a sharp chef's knife to cut off both the bottom and top. Place the celeriac on its even cut surface. Using the chef's knife, slice off the remaining celeriac skin vertically from top to bottom.

Crabapple trees bearing the little golf-ball-size fruits line some of the streets near my home in Toronto's east end. I like to pass them on my daily runs as they effuse a sweet autumn smell in October. Most are harvested at this point and seen at markets, but some are spotted in large grocery store chains as late as December.

Bourbon Sweet Potatoes & Parsnips with Hazelnut Dukkah

Serves 8

Sweet potatoes and parsnips are staple winter vegetables in Ontario and a perfect remedy for our colder climate. In this case, they are glazed in bourbon and topped with a hazelnut dukkah—an Egyptian spice blend of toasted nuts and fragrant spices. Hazelnuts grow plentifully in Ontario—and if you catch sight of them in the fall (like the ones I get from farmer Betsey at the Leslieville Farmers' Market), you will see the beautiful green blossoms that envelop the nuts. When fresh, it is hard not to eat them by the handful, but reserving a few to pair with fennel and enrich this sweet-and-savoury recipe is well worth the restraint. What follows is a charming side dish for your holiday table or alongside my Spice-Rubbed Beef Brisket with Horseradish (page 220).

Bourbon Sweet Potatoes & Parsnips

1 cup (250 mL) extra virgin olive oil

3 tablespoons bourbon

2 tablespoons white wine vinegar

4 medium sweet potatoes (2 pounds/900 grams total), peeled

4 medium parsnips (½ pound/ 225 grams total), peeled

Kosher salt, to season

Hazelnut Dukkah

3 tablespoons hazelnuts

1 teaspoon fennel seeds

½ teaspoon flaky sea salt

Preheat the oven to 400°F (200°C). In a very large mixing bowl, whisk together the oil, bourbon, and vinegar.

Without cutting all the way through, cut the sweet potatoes and parsnips crosswise into ½-inch (1 cm) slices. Arrange the vegetables, still intact at the bottom, into a 7- × 11-inch (18 × 28 cm) baking dish and pour the bourbon mixture over top. Generously season with salt.

Roast the vegetables for 30 minutes. Remove the dish to baste the vegetables with the bourbon liquid collected at the bottom of the dish. Continue to roast until the vegetables are soft and the tops are golden, about 30 minutes more.

While the sweet potatoes and parsnips roast, spread the hazelnuts and fennel seeds evenly across a small baking sheet. Place the baking sheet in the oven and toast the hazelnuts and fennel seeds alongside the sweet potatoes and parsnips for 4 minutes. Set aside to cool. Once the hazelnuts and fennel seeds have cooled, place them, along with the salt, into a mortar and use the pestle to coarsely grind the hazelnuts into smaller pieces and the fennel becomes fragrant. Set the dukkah aside for serving.

Remove the sweet potatoes and parsnips from the oven, sprinkle with the hazelnut dukkah, and serve immediately.

Oyster Mushrooms on Tarragon Butter Linguine

Serves 4

Oyster mushrooms are impeccable solo but will also bring a meaty flavour to whatever dish they find themselves in. My farmer friend Dave, from Kendal Hills Farm, has a constant supply of varying mushrooms, but I keep coming back for the oyster—a soulmate to a butter-bound tarragon linguine. Any oyster mushroom works well here, but it is the smooth-as-a-pearl Snow Fairy variety that Dave harvests at this time of year. Much like its name implies, it has snowy-white wings and the ability to withstand the cold temperatures of Ontario's deep woods in December. There is a gentle beauty in its mild, earthy taste and, in this dish, it is complemented by the sweet anise flavours of tarragon speckled into a glistening plate of creamy almost-melted Mascarpone linguine. A rich dish in both flavour and texture, it seems sensible to deem this a necessary luxury of winter.

2 cups (500 mL) chicken broth (or vegetable broth)

5 tablespoons (75 grams) unsalted butter, room temperature, divided

2 shallots, finely chopped

2 cloves garlic, minced

12 ounces (340 grams) oyster mushrooms (about 4 cups/1 litre)

2 teaspoons chopped fresh tarragon

3 sprigs fresh thyme

Kosher salt and freshly cracked black pepper, to season

½ cup (125 mL) dry white wine

½ pound (225 grams) fresh linguine (see Note)

3 tablespoons mascarpone

¾ cup (2½ ounces/75 grams) freshly grated Parmesan, plus more for serving

2 teaspoons chopped fresh chives, for garnish

In a medium saucepan over medium-low, bring the chicken broth to a simmer. Cover and keep at a simmer until ready to use.

In a large skillet over medium-high, melt 4 tablespoons butter. Add the shallots and sauté, stirring often, until softened, about 4 minutes. Add the garlic and continue to sauté until fragrant, about 2 minutes. Add the mushrooms, tarragon, and thyme. Use a wooden spoon to give the mushrooms a good stir until soft and golden, about 8 minutes. Season with salt and pepper.

Add the linguine to the skillet and cook, stirring, for about 2 minutes. Add the wine, stirring frequently, until the liquid has nearly evaporated, 8 to 10 minutes. Ladle in 1 cup (250 mL) of the hot chicken broth and continue to cook, stirring constantly, until the liquid has fully evaporated. Add more broth, ½ cup (125 mL) at a time, while continuing to stir. This will allow the pasta to absorb the liquid before adding more. The linguine is ready when it is tender and creamy-looking, 10 to 15 minutes from when you started adding the broth. The pasta will be cooked through and have a slight bite to it. Remove the skillet from the heat and discard the stems of the thyme. Stir in the remaining 1 tablespoon butter, the mascarpone, and the Parmesan. Season with salt and pepper. Serve with a garnish of chopped fresh chives and a few extra shavings of Parmesan.

NOTE

Fresh pasta is more tender than dried and best with delicate sauces. The texture of the pasta can take centre stage and is intended to be served al dente and velvety to the touch. Fresh takes about half the time to cook. If fresh pasta isn't available, you can use ½ pound (225 grams) dried linguine instead. If so, before you start cooking the sauce, boil a pot of water seasoned with enough salt to mimic the sea, and cook the linguine for 8 minutes. Remove from the heat and drain. Set the linguine aside and add to the skillet when you would add the fresh linguine.

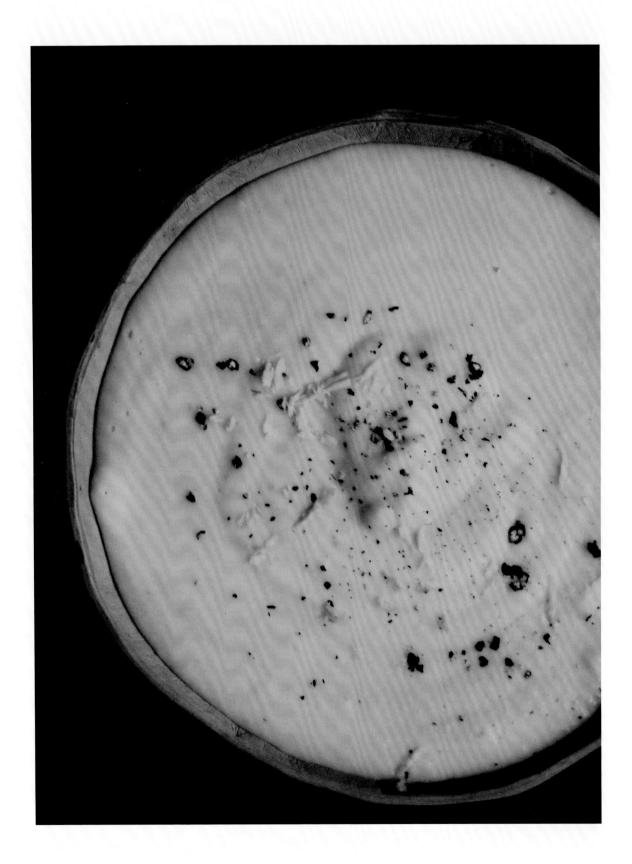

Creamed Celeriac & Potatoes

Serves 4

Celeriac and potatoes are like two peas in a pod (or for the purposes of this recipe, more like two roots in a pot), and they make a wonderful accompaniment to almost any dish in need of a warm embrace (Mustard-Crusted Rack of Lamb on page 52, Apricot BBQ Sticky Ribs on page 136, and Spice-Rubbed Beef Brisket on page 220 are all great options). Celeriac is a real odd-looking vegetable—its skin is a wood-like bark and knobs protrude out of every corner—but it's those knots and eccentricities that make it so beautiful. (Sometimes I like to imagine it is a little moon in my hands.) To make things less intimidating, use a good chef's knife and lob off the skin. Underneath is a nutty, mild, celery-flavoured bulb that transforms into a creamy, fluffy mash, making it an exciting friend to the familiar earthy potato. The addition of freshly shaved horseradish and cracked peppercorns makes for a spurring experience as a side dish.

---

1 pound (450 grams) celeriac, peeled and roughly chopped

1 pound (450 grams) yellow potatoes, peeled and roughly chopped

1½ cups (375 mL) whole milk, plus more if needed

1 tablespoon kosher salt

4 tablespoons (60 grams) unsalted butter, room temperature

2 tablespoons freshly shaven horseradish (optional)

Kosher salt and freshly cracked black pepper

In a large covered saucepan over medium, bring the celeriac, potatoes, milk, and kosher salt to a simmer. Ensure the celeriac and potatoes are submerged in the liquid and simmer until they are tender, about 25 minutes. Add extra milk if the root vegetables are not fully submerged.

Purée the cooked potatoes and celeriac milk mixture in a blender until well incorporated, 1 to 2 minutes at medium speed and gradually increasing to high. Turn off the blender and add the butter and horseradish, if using, and blend on medium, gradually increasing to high until creamy and smooth, about 3 minutes. If at any point you find your potatoes and celeriac sticking to the edges of the blender, turn off the blender and use a spatula to scrape down the edges before continuing to blend to smooth. Taste and season with salt and pepper before serving.

Crispy Duck & Radicchio Salad with Apple & Pickled Turnips
Serves 4

With good direction and quality poultry, you will have the perfect meal to entertain and a duck more delicious than if you were to eat out. It's best to choose a duck breast cased in a layer of its own white fat and one from a butcher with considerate farming practices. Score them, salt them, cook them low enough to render the fat, and then crisp it all up in the oven. A pinky medium-rare duck with crackling, sea salt–flaked skin takes no more than 20 minutes. Sweet apples and pickled turnips make a good accompaniment to balance duck's robust flavours. Crispy duck can be the most intimidating name for a meal made with simplicity and little else to intrude.

Herby Honey Dressing

1 teaspoon mustard seeds

¼ cup (60 mL) white wine vinegar

2 tablespoons honey

1 sprig rosemary

½ teaspoon kosher salt

¼ cup (60 mL) good-quality extra virgin olive oil

2 skin-on duck breasts (3 pounds/ 1.4 kilograms total)

1 tablespoon kosher salt

½ teaspoon freshly cracked black pepper

2 sprigs fresh thyme

2 cloves garlic, thinly sliced

2 cups roughly chopped radicchio leaves

1 apple, cored and sliced into half-moons

½ cup quick pickled turnips (page 184)

To make the dressing, heat a medium skillet over medium-high. Add the mustard seeds and toast until the seeds begin to pop, about 2 minutes. Add the vinegar, honey, rosemary, salt, and olive oil. As soon as bubbles form, reduce the heat to low and simmer until the honey has dissolved, about 3 minutes. Take the skillet off the heat, remove the rosemary sprig, and set aside until ready to serve.

Score the duck breasts on the fatty side. Generously season both sides of the breasts with the salt and black pepper. Set aside at room temperature for at least 30 minutes.

Preheat the oven to 400°F (200°C). Place an oven-safe skillet on the stove and add the duck breasts skin side down. Turn the stove on to medium and slowly sear, rendering the duck fat. (It is important to start with a dry, cool skillet to allow the fat to release, rather than placing the duck in a hot pan and locking the fat in.) After 5 minutes of cooking, add the thyme and garlic and continue to cook for another 10 minutes. Flip the duck breasts skin side up and cook for 1 minute more. Flip the duck breasts once more, skin side down, and roast the duck in the oven: 4 minutes for medium-rare or 6 minutes for medium. Place the cooked duck breasts on a cutting board and let sit for 10 minutes before cutting (to lock in the juices).

Plate the radicchio, apple slices, and pickled turnips. Drizzle the dressing over each plate. Cut the duck breasts into large slices and lay the sliced duck atop the radicchio salad to serve.

Spice-Rubbed Beef Brisket with Horseradish

Serves 8

The sudden drop in temperature in December always pricks my appetite, and as the evenings get longer, I have the opportunity to spend a little more time in the kitchen to tend to my meals. The entire experience of making a brisket is a joy: visiting the butcher; brining the beef for a slow roast; biding one's time with phone calls to friends because slow-cooking puts you under house arrest; and, of course, inviting said friends over for dinner. There is a bit of patience needed—the key to brisket is time. Well, days. (This is a 24-hour-plus recipe.) But when served on a table surrounded by loved ones, you have a meal fit for royalty.

4 pounds (1.8 kilograms) beef brisket

2 tablespoons kosher salt

1 tablespoon brown sugar

2 teaspoons caraway seeds

2 teaspoons garlic powder

2 tablespoons extra virgin olive oil, divided

1 large yellow onion, thinly sliced

3 cloves garlic, minced

2 cups (500 mL) Bone Broth (page 248)

½ cup (125 mL) dry red wine

3 bay leaves

1 teaspoon freshly cracked black pepper

Freshly grated horseradish (optional)

One Day before Serving: Dry-brine the brisket with a good rubbing of salt, brown sugar, caraway seeds, and garlic powder. Cover in a sealed container and store in the refrigerator for 24 hours. This allows the meat to take on many flavours and tenderizes it for that melt-in-your-mouth feel.

Day of Serving: Lightly coat a large (7-quart/6¾-litre) Dutch oven or oven-safe lidded skillet with 1 tablespoon oil and heat over medium-high. Add the brisket to sear, 7 to 10 minutes per side. Once seared, set aside.

Preheat the oven to 375°F (190°C). Re-coat the Dutch oven with the remaining 1 tablespoon oil and sauté the onions over medium. Cook until golden brown, about 15 minutes. Add the garlic and cook until fragrant, 2 to 3 minutes. Add the bone broth, wine, and bay leaves. Increase the heat to high and bring to a boil. Once boiling, reduce heat to low and cozy the brisket back into the pot, fat top facing up (this allows the fat to melt into the rest of the beef, tenderizing the meat). If the liquid does not reach halfway up the brisket, add a little more broth. Cover with a lid and cook in the oven for 2 hours and 15 minutes. Take the brisket out of the oven and remove the lid, then return to the oven to cook for another 45 minutes.

Your brisket is done when it's tender with a thick, glossy layer of spice-rubbed bark. The centre of the brisket should reach 195°F (91°C) on an instant-read thermometer.

Set aside to cool for at least 1 hour before cutting (see Note). Top with the horseradish if desired.

When buying brisket, choose veiny cuts with a thick layer of fat on one side.

It is important that the brisket sits for 1 to 2 hours before you cut into it. This will ensure the brisket is extra tender.

Cranberry Horseradish Linzer Cookies

Makes 12(ish) cookies

Linzer cookies are a traditional Christmas cookie from Linz, Austria, popularized in Canada because of the growing devotion to the annual cookie exchange between friends and family members. Two-layered short-crust cookies with sweet jam peeking out and dusted with powdery sugar, these will most definitely be making an appearance in my cookie tins this year (as they have every other year). But first let's address the elephant in the room: that is, the perplexing notion that horseradish could find its place in dessert. (Who says that a winter root whose pungency will wake up every nerve in your body should be reduced to one role as a condiment for meats and fish?) However absurd it may seem, horseradish is a sharp friend that can accentuate the sweet tang of cranberry jam.

2¼ cups (280 grams) all-purpose flour

¾ teaspoon kosher salt

½ cup (100 grams) granulated sugar

1 cup + 2 tablespoons (270 grams) unsalted butter, room temperature, cut into 1-inch (2.5 cm) pieces

1 egg

⅔ cup (160 mL) cranberry jam (or blackcurrant or cherry jam)

1 tablespoon freshly grated horseradish

1 cup (130 grams) powdered sugar, for dusting

NOTES

If you don't have a stand mixer, you can also use a large bowl with a handheld electric mixer.

Cut the dough nice and thin (no thicker than ⅛ inch/3 mm) to keep the treats stackable and to avoid hefty, dry cookies.

In a medium mixing bowl, whisk the flour and salt to combine. In a stand mixer fitted with the paddle attachment, combine the sugar and butter (see Note). Beat on medium speed into a smooth batter. Add the egg and beat to combine. Reduce the speed to low and gradually add the dry ingredients, ½ cup at a time. Beat until a dough has formed. Remove the bowl from the mixer and use your hands to knead the dough a couple of times to work in any dry bits neglected at the bottom of the bowl. Divide the dough in half and roll into two 9-inch (23 cm) long logs. Wrap each log tightly in plastic wrap and chill until firm, about 2 hours.

In a small mixing bowl, mix the cranberry jam with the horseradish. Set aside for the cookie assembly.

Line two large baking sheets with parchment paper. Place one oven rack in the upper third level and one on the lower third level of the oven. Preheat the oven to 350°F (175°C).

Remove the rolls of dough from the refrigerator and unwrap. Slice the dough into ⅛ inch (3 mm) thick rounds (see Note), rotating the log every few slices to keep its shape. Place the cookies 2 inches (5 cm) apart on the prepared baking sheets. Use a cookie cutter to punch out the centres of half the cookies (centres can be baked as taste-tester scraps if you so please). Bake the cookies, rotating baking sheets back to front and front to back midway through to get an even bake, until the cookies are golden around the edges but still pale in the centre, 12 to 16 minutes. Transfer the cookies to wire racks to cool.

Once cool, spread about ¾ teaspoon of the cranberry horseradish jam across the entire surface of each unpunched cookie. Before placing the cut-out top cookies on the now jam-glossed cookies, dust the tops of the cut-out cookies with powdered sugar. Set the powdered cookies, sugar side up, on top of the jammy cookies. Cookies taste best served fresh but can be stored in a sealed container in the refrigerator for up to 7 days.

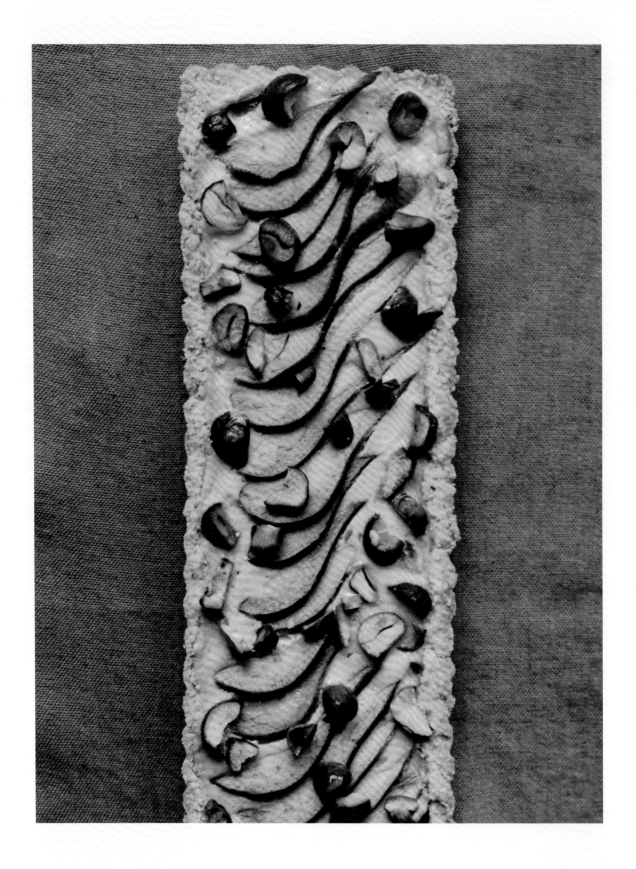

Pear Custard Tart with Roasted Chestnuts

Makes one 5- × 14-inch (12 × 36 cm) tart

A good way to finish an elegant dinner in December is with a cookie-crumbled tart, sliced and warmed enough so that each blistered pear falls kindly into the ivory, velvet depths of crème fraîche. Roasted chestnuts pop as they sweeten in the oven—just the right amount of a toasty holiday nudge—to what is already a seasonal dessert. As kids, we used to collect chestnuts from the playground up the street. I don't think we ever ate them, which is a shame because the American chestnut tree is a bit of a rarity in Ontario these days, but a few farms in Ontario grow and harvest chestnuts for the holiday season. They can be found at most grocery stores as a holiday staple, along with crispy bell-shaped pears—light green beacons of hope when most fruits are no longer in season. You can enjoy your tart freshly baked or sliced cold for breakfast, in all of its nutty, custardy delight.

½ cup (125 mL) crème fraîche

1 egg, lightly beaten

2 tablespoons granulated sugar

1 teaspoon pure vanilla extract

¼ teaspoon pure almond extract

1 tablespoon all-purpose flour (or gluten-free flour blend; see Note, page 148), sifted

1 batch Forgiving Flaky Tart Crust (page 180)

2 ripe Bosc pears, cored and thinly sliced

⅓ cup chestnuts, roasted and roughly chopped, for garnish

Preheat the oven to 350°F (175°C). Lightly butter a 5- × 14-inch (12 × 36 cm) tart pan (it is ideal to have a tart pan with a release notch or removable surface for serving).

To make the filling, in a medium bowl, whisk together the crème fraîche, egg, sugar, and vanilla and almond extracts. Add the flour and stir until smooth.

Prepare the tart crust (page 180, steps 2 and 3).

Pour the crème fraîche filling into the par-baked tart shell and neatly arrange the pear slices on top. Bake the tart at 350°F (175°C) until the filling has set and the fruit is tender, 25 to 30 minutes. Transfer the tart to a wire rack to cool slightly before releasing the tart from its pan.

Just before serving, garnish with roasted chestnuts. When it comes to a pear custard tart, it is rare to have leftovers, but in the event that this happens, the tart can be sealed in an airtight container and chilled for up to 3 days.

How To: Make Sauerkraut

Makes 6 to 8 cups (1.5 to 2 litres)

Who determines, and for what strange reason, the social status of a vegetable? Despite its poor PR, in my home, cabbage is considered one of the most precious plants. It is the grandfather of all cruciferous vegetables: as old as the day is long, it keeps for ages, delivers an impressive dose of vitamins, and—when fermented—is one of the best gifts for your gut. Often the last one standing in fields covered in frost under grey skies, it's cheap and hardy to sustain all throughout the hunger gap (between January to March). It is a survival vegetable, yet I have heard groans about the never-ending cabbage in some people's refrigerators ("I don't know how to use it"), which is a strange complaint. For one, cabbage can last forever (up to 2 months in the refrigerator), and second, it is a very versatile vegetable. Throughout the winter, I am roasting, butter-basting, stir-frying, steaming, or slawing cabbage. So, yeah, I guess you'd say I've got a shtick about cabbage and would love if everyone else could give it the attention it deserves.

Making sauerkraut is something of an inherited skill from my Ukrainian grandmother. Her basement was lined with glass jars of pickles and fermented vegetables all swimming in her fermentation crocks—which were the size of a drum set. Her devotion to a good fermentation has been inscribed into my bones. If you ask me how to eat sauerkraut, I will say straight out of the jar or on any dish that needs a bit more life. For more appropriate advice, the following is how I make sauerkraut.

Equipment

1 food processor, fitted with the shredding blade (or 1 chef's knife)

1 large mixing bowl

2 to 3 large, clean wide-mouth jars with lids (each 3 cups/750 mL)

1 wooden spoon

2 to 3 small jars (each 1 cup/250 mL)

Pie weights (optional)

Paper towel

Sauerkraut

1 medium red cabbage (2 to 3 pounds/900 grams to 1.4 kilograms), quartered and inner core removed (see Note)

4 to 6 teaspoons kosher salt

2 tablespoons coriander seeds

2 tablespoons dill seeds

Step 1: Use a food processor fitted with the shredding blade or a sharp chef's knife to cut the cabbage into very thin strips. This will result in about 12 to 16 cups (3 to 4 litres) of shredded cabbage.

Step 2: Place the cabbage strips in a large bowl and sprinkle 4 teaspoons salt over the cabbage. Let the cabbage sit for 10 to 15 minutes to release its juices. Depending on the size of your cabbage, you may need to add 1 to 2 more teaspoons salt. If you find that the cabbage is on the larger side (3 pounds/1.4 kilograms, about the size of a child's basketball) and is not releasing juice as it sits, add more salt, 1 teaspoon at a time.

Step 3: Squeeze the cabbage in fistfuls to bruise and encourage the cabbage to release more of its juices. Continue for 5 to 10 minutes.

Step 4: Add the coriander and dill seeds. Mix to combine.

recipe continues

Choose a head of cabbage that is heavy for its size and has crisp, firm, packed leaves. Purple, green, or savoy cabbage all work well here.

Do not be scared of mould. Sauerkraut has this magical way of protecting itself with natural antibiotics. Mould shows up only in areas above water, so submerge every last bit of cabbage before fermenting. If the mould appears only at the top of your jar, scrape out the mould and any lingering mouldy bits with a spoon. Add more salt water, ensuring that every last bit of cabbage is submerged in the liquid.

Coriander and dill are what I love to add to my sauerkraut, but this is your chance to go wild and try new things (mustard seeds, cumin seeds, shredded carrots for colour, or whatever whole spice your eye spies in your kitchen cupboard).

Step 5: Transfer the cabbage mixture and its liquid to the 3-cup (750 mL) jars. Use your fists or a wooden spoon to press down firmly on the cabbage. The cabbage needs to be jam-packed.

Step 6: By now, the cabbage will fill anywhere from 2 to 2½ cups (500 to 675 mL) per jar. If you still don't have enough natural brine to cover all the cabbage, mix ¼ teaspoon salt in 1 cup (250 mL) water and pour over the cabbage until completely submerged.

Step 7: Now that you have pressed the sauerkraut down, there will be spare room to top the sauerkraut jars with the smaller 1-cup (250 mL) jars. Add pie weights or water to the small jars to add pressure. Cover the top of the jars with a paper towel and screw on the sealing band. This will stop any outside particles from entering the sauerkraut but will still allow the aerobic process to continue. You may use your snap lids to close the jars, but do not seal tight. Trust me, from experience, this ends in a tie-die sauerkraut explosion.

Step 8: Store the sauerkraut in a dark place (like a cupboard) at room temperature for 3 to 4 weeks. Check in every few days. As sauerkraut ferments, it develops its own good bacteria that kills off harmful bacteria entering its environment. If there is a layer of scum on the top, this is an indication that there is too much air in the jar, so simply remove the scum and add more brine.

Step 9: When you've achieved your desired tenderness and pungency of sauerkraut, seal the jar with the jar's original lid and store in the refrigerator. Sauerkraut will last for up to 3 months refrigerated. Serve as a condiment or eat on its own.

Acorn Squash & Blue Cheese on Red Fife Parathas
Serves 4

A paratha—a layered flatbread from India—is quite delicious on its own but I spent a lot of my week-ends eating these at my childhood best friend's home with an extra pat of butter to drip into each layer of flakiness. Though not traditional, I like to think they can even handle a mélange of flavours—the peppery sautéed garlic greens, the sweet, tender flesh of an acorn squash, and a sharp nip of blue cheese—and you have yourself a first-class ticket to flavour city.

Red Fife Parathas

1 cup (130 grams) sifted red fife flour (see Note)

1 cup (125 grams) all-purpose flour, plus more for dusting

1 teaspoon kosher salt

7 tablespoons extra virgin olive oil, divided

½ cup (125 mL) lukewarm water, plus more if needed

2 cloves garlic, minced

3 tablespoons ghee (or canola oil), to coat parathas

Squash & Garlic Greens

1 acorn squash (12 ounces to 1 pound/340 to 450 grams), seeds removed and cut into 1-inch (2.5 cm) wedges

2 tablespoons extra virgin olive oil, divided

Kosher salt, to season

6 cloves garlic, minced

2 cups roughly chopped dandelion greens (or chard, kale, or purslane)

2 tablespoons crumbled blue cheese (or chèvre), for garnish

Good-quality extra virgin olive oil, for serving

Make the Red Fife Parathas: In a large bowl, mix the red fife flour, all-purpose flour, and salt. Add 1 tablespoon olive oil. While mixing the dough with your hand, slowly add the water to achieve a dough-like consistency that can be shaped in your hands. If the dough crumbles, add more water, 1 teaspoon at a time.

On a clean work surface, knead the dough for 5 minutes until smooth. Divide the dough into six pieces. Use your hands to roll each piece into a golf-ball-size ball and place back in the bowl. Lightly coat with olive oil and cover with a damp towel. Refrigerate the dough balls for 15 minutes.

Dust a work surface with flour. Coat one ball in all-purpose flour and roll it out with a rolling pin to form a thin round, about ¹⁄₁₆ inch (1 mm) thick. The round does not need to be a perfect circle. With a small sharp knife, cut ½-inch (1 cm) strips; you should have about 10 to 12 strips. Sprinkle 1 teaspoon minced garlic and 1 tablespoon olive oil on the strips. At this point, the strips are beside one another on the counter. Push the strips all together into one aggregate mass and wrap them around your hand like you are a boxer wrapping your hands with tape (this will allow the strips to intertwine together, creating flaky pockets when rolled out and cooked). Roll the wrapped strips out one last time to flatten into an 8-inch (20 cm) diameter round and set aside. Repeat with the remaining five balls of dough, resulting in six parathas altogether.

recipe continues

Heat a dry skillet over medium. One at a time, cook the parathas for 3 minutes on each side. After the allotted time, brush the top side of the paratha with ghee and flip. Brush the other side with ghee and continue to cook for 1 minute. Flip once more and cook for 1 minute more. By this time, your parathas will be a golden colour and soft and flaky in the middle. Remove from the heat, wrap in a clean tea towel, and continue with the remaining parathas.

Make the Squash & Garlic Greens: Preheat the oven to 450°F (230°C) and line a baking sheet with parchment paper. In a large mixing bowl, toss the squash with 1 tablespoon olive oil and a generous pinch of salt. Place the squash on the prepared baking sheet and roast for 30 minutes, until pieces are fork-tender. For even roasting, remove the baking sheet from the oven at the 15-minute mark to flip the squash. Set aside.

Coat a medium-size skillet with 1 tablespoon olive oil and set over medium-low heat. Once the oil begins to shimmer, add the garlic. Sauté the garlic, stirring frequently, until fragrant, 1 to 2 minutes. Add the dandelion greens and continue to sauté for 3 minutes. Remove the greens and garlic from the heat and set aside for serving.

Assemble the Parathas: Plate the parathas and add two wedges of squash. Divide the greens among the parathas. Garnish with the blue cheese and a drizzle of good-quality olive oil.

NOTE: *Red fife is a heritage grain and one of Canada's oldest cereal crops. If you can't find red fife flour, seek out another finely milled whole grain instead, like spelt.*

Puffy Oat Oladyi (Ukrainian Pancakes)

Serves 4

Oladyi are small, thick Ukrainian pancakes reminiscent of buttermilk pancakes, but fluffier and less cakey. They are fried in a bit more oil than your standard pancakes, which puffs them up—like a good-quality down winter jacket, both toasty and warming. The magic ingredient here is the cultured milk known as kefir. The result is a tart and pillowy pancake that requires little gilding. Traditionally, a dollop of smetana—a sweet, silky sauce that often belongs on desserts—is served with oladyi, but I like to eat them plain or soaked in a little maple syrup. A pat of butter melting on the top, catching each pancake's craggy edges as it glides down the stack, is also not a bad idea.

1¼ cups (110 grams) rolled oats

½ teaspoon kosher salt

1 teaspoon baking soda

2 eggs

2 cups (500 mL) plain kefir (or buttermilk)

2 tablespoons pure maple syrup, plus more for serving

¼ cup (60 mL) canola oil, for frying

Butter, for serving

In a blender, blend the oats and salt until a flour consistency has formed, 1 to 2 minutes. Add the baking soda, then give the blender a quick blitz to mix everything well.

In a large mixing bowl, lightly beat the eggs, then whisk in the kefir and maple syrup. Pour in the oat mixture from the blender and whisk to combine. Don't over-whisk—a few lumps are to be expected. Set the mixture aside and let the batter sit untouched for 15 minutes.

While you are waiting for the batter to thicken, you can begin to heat a large skillet over medium heat. Add enough oil to slick the surface, and reduce the heat to medium-low. Use a ladle or large spoon to drop about ¼ cup (60 mL) of the oladyi batter into the hot oil, filling the skillet with as many pancakes as comfortably fit (don't overcrowd the pan). Fry on one side until bubbles form on top and the bottom side is golden brown, 3 to 4 minutes. With a spatula, gently flip the oladyi to avoid the splash of hot oil. Adjust the heat as necessary to keep the oladyi from browning too quickly. The oladyi will puff up as soon as you flip them over and continue to cook. (If you find the skillet is getting too dry, add a little more oil as needed.) A properly cooked oladyi will spring back when lightly poked.

Serve them as they come out of the pan or place the cooked oladyi on a plate loosely covered with a clean tea towel and repeat the process until all oladyi are ready to be enjoyed with a pat of butter and doused in maple syrup.

Farmer's Cheese & Sautéed Mushrooms with a Toasted Italian Loaf

Serves 4

One of the gifts of winter produce is the onion. I think most people take onions for granted because they are always available and in "peak season," but what would we do without onions? They're the backbone of many dishes, adding depth and mellowness to our home cooking. In this dish, a combination of leeks and Vidalia onions cooked in a brown butter add creaminess and caramel sweetness to sautéed mushrooms and black garlic—building an umami savouriness that some vegetarian dishes miss. The sauerkraut finishes things off, adding vibrancy and contrast to what would be a nice but not nearly as invigorating dish. Serve with a fresh loaf of bread, of any sort, cut open to expose its cloud-soft textures and crusty edges, and toast to support a cargo of pleasing winter flavours.

Fried Garlic Capers

1 tablespoon extra virgin olive oil

1 clove garlic, minced

2 tablespoons capers

1 tablespoon unsalted butter, room temperature

1 Vidalia onion, thinly sliced

1 cup (40 grams) cremini mushrooms, scrubbed and quartered

2 cloves black garlic, pressed with a spoon into a purée (see Note)

1 leek, end trimmed and dark green tops removed, thinly sliced into rounds, and washed thoroughly

Flaky sea salt or finishing salt

4 slices fresh Italian bread

12 ounces (340 grams) Farmer's Cheese (page 115)

2 tablespoons Sauerkraut (page 227), chopped

Good-quality extra virgin olive oil, for drizzling

In a medium skillet over medium-high, heat the oil. Add the garlic and sauté until fragrant, 1 to 2 minutes. Add the capers and stir until crisp, 3 to 4 minutes. Remove from the heat and set aside for serving.

Preheat the oven to 350°F (175°C). In a skillet over medium-high, melt the butter. Once the butter begins to bubble, reduce the heat to medium and add the onions. Sauté until golden, about 10 minutes. Add the mushrooms, black garlic, and leeks. Continue to cook until the mushrooms wilt and the leeks become transparent, 5 to 6 minutes. Remove the skillet from the heat, season with salt, and set aside.

Toast the bread in the oven for 2 minutes or until lightly crisp. Set aside for serving but keep the oven on.

Place the farmer's cheese in a baking dish and warm it in the oven for 5 minutes.

Divide the farmer's cheese among four dishes, placing it in the centre of each dish. Then divide the mushroom and onion mixture among the plates, surrounding the cheese. Sprinkle with fried garlic capers and sauerkraut and top with a drizzle of oil. Serve with a basket of the toasted bread.

NOTE: *Black garlic is an aged garlic with sweet, squishy, umami depth, and one of my favourite additions to a vegetarian dish. We can thank the culinary techniques of Korea for this slow-roasted flavour.*

Thick Tomato Cannellini Soup with Ribbed Kale

Serves 4

Of all the nostalgic recipes I have made in my life, this is a warm embrace to cold, snowy Januaries. It is a soup to warm the insides and nourish the soul. Between the slow-cooked onions, garlic, black garlic, and shiitake mushrooms, the aromatics are at prime umami level. There are two keys to this soup's comforts: First, just as you would for the Italian ribollita version, you must use lacinato kale. This slightly bitter, pleasingly humble ribbed winter green adds depth and substance. When cut into long, thin strips, it wilts into the soup and results in soft ribbons. Second, serve the soup hot—not so hot that you burn your tongue, but hot enough that you feel it in your chest.

2 tablespoons extra virgin olive oil, plus more for drizzling (optional)

2 yellow onions, diced

3 cloves garlic, minced

3 cloves black garlic (see Note, page 62)

2½ cups (675 grams) shiitake mushrooms, stems removed and diced

1 can (28 ounces/796 mL) whole tomatoes

3 tablespoons tomato paste

2 bay leaves

4 sprigs fresh thyme

4 cups (1 litre) low-sodium chicken broth

Kosher salt and freshly cracked black pepper, to season

1 can (28 ounces/796 mL) cannellini beans, rinsed and drained

1 bunch lacinato kale, coarsely chopped (4 to 6 cups/1 to 1.5 litres)

1 rustic loaf of bread, for serving

Heat a large Dutch oven or heavy pot on the stove over medium-low. Add the oil, and wait 1 minute or so to let the pot heat up (you can test this by flicking a dribble of water onto the pan and if it sizzles it's hot enough). Now add the onions. Cook until the onions are translucent and blond, 10 to 15 minutes, stirring every so often. Add the garlic, black garlic, and mushrooms. Continue to cook until the garlic is fragrant and the mushrooms begin to gloss and wilt, stirring every few minutes, about 7 minutes. Add the tomatoes, tomato paste, bay leaves, thyme, broth, and a generous seasoning of salt and pepper. Give it all a good stir.

Bring the entire pot to a rolling boil, then reduce to a simmer. Let the soup simmer for 40 minutes, then add the beans and kale. Continue to cook for another 5 minutes or so, until you are ready to serve. Taste and season with salt if needed.

Serve in large bowls with rustic ripped bread. Sometimes a little olive oil spooned over the soup is nice too.

Winter Wheat Berry Salad

Serves 4

Za'atar has a magical way of bringing any dish together. In this recipe, for instance, there is a toffee-like sweetness that comes from the Japanese yam, the lemony zing of fresh sorrel, and the nuttiness of the wheat berry. In what otherwise would be a cacophony of flavours, za'atar unites the ingredients. If roasted potatoes are not enough to make this a hearty winter salad, a warm base of wheat berries certainly will. I'd be remiss not to mention our winter MVP, the pear—juicy, sweet, and a fruit we can trust to be there no matter how low the temperature drops.

Lemon Honey Dressing

¼ cup (60 mL) walnut oil (see Note)

Juice of 1 lemon (zest the lemon first though, you'll need it later)

1 tablespoon liquid honey

Kosher salt and freshly cracked black pepper, to season

Winter Wheat Berry Salad

1 large (1½ pounds/680 grams) Japanese yam, scrubbed and cut into 1-inch (2.5 cm) cubes

2 tablespoons grapeseed oil

1 tablespoon za'atar

½ teaspoon kosher salt, plus more to season wheat berries

½ cup wheat berries, rinsed and dried

1 tablespoon apple cider vinegar

¼ cup raw almonds

6 cups sorrel or bunched spinach, chiffonade (see Note)

1 Bosc pear, thinly sliced

Zest of 1 lemon

In a small bowl, whisk together the oil, lemon juice, honey, salt, and pepper. Set aside.

Preheat the oven to 375°F (190°C) and line a baking sheet with parchment paper. In a large bowl, coat the Japanese yams with the grapeseed oil. Season with the za'atar and ½ teaspoon salt. Toss to coat and spread the yams evenly across the prepared baking sheet. Roast for 30 to 35 minutes, until the bottom edges crisp up and toffee-like juices ooze around the yams. Set aside for serving, reserving the baking sheet and keeping the oven on.

In a small pot on high, bring 1½ cups (375 mL) water to a boil. Once the water is boiling, reduce the heat to medium-low and add the wheat berries, vinegar, and a pinch of salt. Simmer until the wheat berries are cooked (they will be soft with a bit of chew to them), 30 to 35 minutes. Drain the wheat berries and give them a gentle shake to allow excess liquid to drain out.

Place the almonds on the same lined baking sheet used for the yams and toast in the oven for 5 to 6 minutes. Once toasted, set them on a separate plate to cool. Once cooled, give them a rough chop.

Toss the greens with three-quarters of the dressing in a large bowl. Plate the dressed greens. Top with pear slices, roasted yams, and warm wheat berries. This will give a light wilt to the greens. Drizzle the remaining dressing over the salad. Sprinkle with the toasted almonds and lemon zest before serving.

NOTES

Grown in Canada, walnuts add a delicate flavour to a dish, as does their oil. If you do not have walnut oil on hand, though, a good-quality olive oil is your next best friend for the dressing.

Sorrel is a leafy green, similar to spinach but with a lemony tang. Though it grows in Ontario, it can be a bit hard to find in stores. Most farmers' markets and grocery stores that focus on local produce will carry it.

The wheat berry is the whole grain form of wheat, with all three parts (wheat germ, bran, and endosperm) intact.

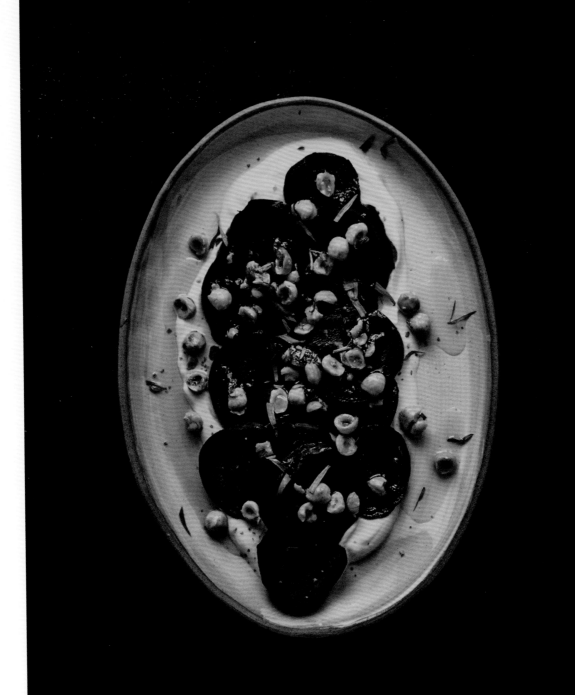

Smoked Beet Carpaccio with Yogurt, Hazelnuts & Tarragon
Serves 4

This beet carpaccio is a plate of smoked beets sliced paper-thin to resemble a traditional beef carpaccio. Peak-season Detroit Dark Red beets have a savoury quality when smoked that marries well with honeyed crunchy hazelnuts and a lift of creamy yogurt. The set-up for this will take a little effort, but after your steamer-smoker-wok concoction has been securely set in place, prepare to collect dividends from this elegant and cheering dish on a grey winter's day.

4 medium red beets, sliced paper-thin

1½ teaspoons kosher salt, plus more to season

1½ tablespoons walnut oil (see Note, page 89), divided

¼ cup hazelnuts, halved and toasted

2 tablespoons honey

½ cup (125 mL) plain 2% yogurt

2 to 3 sprigs fresh tarragon, torn (about 3 to 4 tablespoons), for garnish

In a large bowl, combine the beets and salt.

Line the inside of a wok with two long sheets of foil (about 2 to 3 feet/60 to 90 cm) in a cross shape. The foil will extend beyond the wok like wings and eventually be folded back over everything. Fill the foiled wok with a handful of hickory chips (see Glossary on page 266). Place a 10-inch (25 cm) bamboo steamer on top of the smoking chips. Evenly spread the beets in the steamer. To ensure beets smoke evenly, avoid layering beets on top of one another. This may mean repeating the process a few times. Cover the steamer with its lid and wrap with the extended foil wings from the wok. Add more foil if the entire lid is not covered. This will lock in the smoke and help cook everything evenly. Heat the wok over medium-high for 2 to 3 minutes. Reduce to low and allow the beets to smoke for another 5 to 6 minutes. Remove from the heat and let sit, covered, for 5 minutes to continue to infuse the beets. Unpeel the foil lock, take off the steamer lid, and set beets aside for serving. Repeat this process with the remaining beets, if necessary.

Heat a medium skillet over medium-low. Add 1 tablespoon walnut oil, the hazelnuts, and the honey. Use a wooden spoon to mix well. Cook for 1 to 2 minutes, until the hazelnuts lightly brown. Turn the heat off and add the remaining ½ tablespoon walnut oil. Remove the hazelnut mixture from the skillet and set aside for serving.

Spread 2 tablespoons yogurt across each of four plates. Layer with beet slices and drizzle the hazelnut mixture over top. Season with salt and garnish with tarragon before serving.

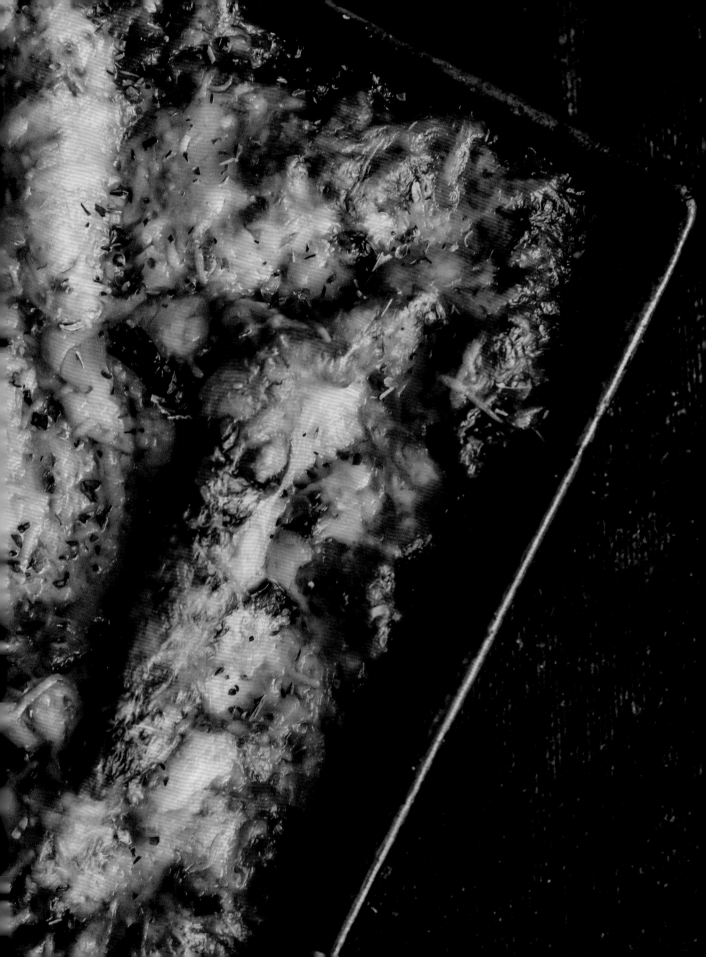

Lasagna al Ragu

Serves 8

As with many pasta recipes, there are a number of variations for lasagna. There is much debate about which cheeses and sauces make a "true" lasagna. I see this unbounded dish as an opportunity for creative expression. For me, I like to sub out the béchamel sauce for a mix of complementary cheeses that make me feel like I am getting a warm hug from my best friend's nona. Pick a sharp Cheddar along with the type of mozzarella that gives a satisfying pull when lifting a square of lasagna out of the pan, and use a strong cheese like Parmesan to sprinkle on top.

This lasagna is a perfect weekend activity for January and will fill your home with the enticing smell of garlicky tomato sauce, and a bubbling mess of crispy brown cheese. It's patience that delivers the full flavour here. This dish is at its best when cooked slowly and tucked into the refrigerator for a good night's rest. Lasagna is even better the second or third day, once the noodles have had a chance to absorb all the flavours. No matter the day you choose to serve your lasagna, eat with abandon and enjoy every last bite.

Ragu

1 tablespoon extra virgin olive oil

1 onion, finely chopped

3 cloves garlic, minced

1 pound (450 grams) lean ground beef

3 tablespoons tomato paste

1 wineglass full of dry white wine (about 1 to 1½ cups/250 to 375 mL, depending on how much you sip)

Kosher salt and freshly cracked black pepper

2 bay leaves

2 tablespoons dried oregano

2 tablespoons fennel seeds

1 can (28 ounces/796 mL) whole tomatoes

1½ cups (375 mL) beef broth (or water)

Make the Ragu: Coat a deep, wide saucepan with the oil and heat over low, then add the onions and gently sauté until transparent. Add the garlic and cook for 2 to 3 minutes more, until fragrant. Add the beef and stir to brown evenly, about 10 minutes. Add the tomato paste and white wine, season to taste with salt and pepper, and add the bay leaves, oregano, and fennel seeds. Give everything a good stir. Add the canned tomatoes a couple at a time, crushing them with your hands as you place them in the pan (or add them in one fell swoop and smash them on the side of the saucepan to help break them down into the sauce). Add the beef broth and give everything one more big stir, then cover to simmer on low for 30 to 40 minutes. Discard the bay leaves once the sauce is ready to go on the assembly line.

recipe continues

Lasagna

6 to 8 sheets fresh lasagna noodles (or dry, see Note)

4 cups (12 ounces/320 grams) shredded mozzarella

2 cups (8 ounces/220 grams) shredded sharp Cheddar

1 cup (3½ ounces/100 grams) freshly grated Parmesan

Make the Lasagna: Preheat the oven to 375°F (190°C).

To assemble the lasagna, begin with a 5½ × 7½-inch (13 × 19 cm) casserole dish that is 2 inches (5 cm) deep. Ladle in two large scoops of the ragu and spread evenly across the bottom of the dish. Layer on three to four lasagna sheets and spread two more ladles of ragu over the noodles. Layer on half of the mozzarella and half of the sharp Cheddar. Repeat layering everything once more (ragu, noodles, and cheese). Finish by sprinkling the Parmesan over the lasagna.

Bake the lasagna for 35 to 40 minutes, until you have a lovely golden, bubbling top. Let cool for at least 30 minutes before serving (the pasta will absorb excess liquid and make for easier cutting), or store, well covered, in the refrigerator for up to 3 days.

NOTE: *Boxed dry lasagna sheets also work well in this recipe. Unlike fresh pasta, you do need to cook dry lasagna before assembling the lasagna; simply follow the instructions on the box. As a rule of thumb, fresh pasta absorbs flavours deeply, while boxed pasta carries the sauce firmly.*

Granny Slowey Apple Pie

Makes one 9-inch (23 cm) pie

This recipe brings back so many flooding memories of childhood, mostly sitting on the kitchen counter watching my mom peel and core bundles of apples. She would prep a large batch of pies to freeze for the next few months—in the event that we had someone to visit, we would never show up empty-handed. She would pull out a pie from the freezer, heat the oven, and within an hour we were blessed with the intoxicating smell of buttery crust and baked apples—dessert done and dusted (see Note). More important were the stories she would tell me about making apple pies as a child with her mom—back home in a little town in Ireland, they called them apple tarts. She, too, would sit in the kitchen at 4 years of age watching my grandmother bake this very pie. When I eat this pie, it brings me much joy to know that my ancestors shared the same pleasant experience of warm apples swaddled in a flaky, tender pastry.

---

1 cup (125 grams) all-purpose flour

¼ cup (60 grams) cold unsalted butter, cut into cubes, plus 1 extra knob, divided

¼ cup (50 grams) lard, room temperature

⅛ teaspoon kosher salt

¼ cup (60 mL) ice water

6 Empire apples (or another tart apple; see Note), peeled, cored, and sliced

2 tablespoons granulated sugar

1 teaspoon milk

Custard or ice cream, for serving (optional)

In a large mixing bowl with an electric mixer, or in a stand mixer fitted with the paddle attachment, combine the flour, ¼ cup (60 grams) butter, lard, and salt and mix on low speed for 1 to 2 minutes, until a shaggy, breadcrumb-like consistency has been reached. Gradually add the ice water and continue to mix on low to form a ball of dough (it is okay if the ball is not perfectly smooth). Split the dough in half (one half will be for the bottom crust, the other will be for the top crust) and wrap each half in plastic wrap. Set in the refrigerator for 20 minutes to chill before rolling out.

Preheat the oven to 350°F (175°C).

Sprinkle flour over your rolling pin and the first ball of chilled dough. On a well-floured surface, roll the dough out into a thick circle, fold three times (like a letter about to be sealed in an envelope), and then reroll the dough out into a 10-inch (25 cm) circle (about ½ inch/1 cm thick). Gently set the circle into a 9-inch (23 cm) pie dish (use a fancy pie dish because you will be serving this straight from the pan). The pastry may flow over the edges of the pie dish. If this is the case, lift the pan and use a paring knife to trim the edges until the dough neatly hugs the pan. Reserve the trimmed cuttings for the not-yet-rolled ball of dough.

recipe continues

Tart apples hold up best in a baked pie. The Empire apples in this pie are considered winter apples. These are the apples (along with Granny Smith, Braeburn, and GoldRush) that are picked late in the season (late October, early November) and will stay fresh right through the spring. They are tart and juicy, and they sweeten over time. Winter apples are, coincidentally, the best apples for swaddling in a warm crust and baking.

Make sure not to overdo it with the milk glaze, as too much can harden the crust. You want just a light gloss.

Scatter the apple slices into the pie shell, filling the pie higher than the brim and letting the apples overflow like a dome. Sprinkle the apples with the sugar and place the knob of butter on top of the apples at the centre.

Add the trimmed dough cuttings from the bottom pie shell to the remaining chilled pastry. Shape the pastry into a ball and lightly flour both the dough and the rolling pin. Roll out on a clean floured surface into a thick circle, fold three times (again, like a letter about to be sealed in an envelope), and reroll the dough out into a 10-inch (25.5 cm) circle (about ½ inch/1 cm thick). Gently set the dough circle on top of the apples. Press the edges of the top and bottom pastry shells together with either your finger and thumb or with a fork. Poke the top centre of the pie crust with a fork three or four times (to let steam escape). Use a pastry brush to glaze the top of the pie pastry with milk (see Note).

Bake the pie for 45 to 60 minutes. You will know it is ready when the pastry is golden brown on the top and your entire home has an intoxicating smell of baked apples and butter. Serve straight from the dish on its own or with a little custard or ice cream.

How To: Make Bone Broth

Makes 8 to 11 cups (2 to 2½ litres)

A winter broth is self-care. It solves every question and soothes every ill . . . or that is how it feels in the moment. What it tangibly does do is warm and satiate, and that is worth its weight in gold on a cold day. Such a broth is immensely useful in the kitchen, either on its own as a restorative snack or as a base for heartier recipes. I slowly cook the bones with a few aromatics—herbs, garlic, onions (stems, peels, and all)—and whatever vegetable is wilting in the back of the crisper drawer (see Note). Once everything has been tossed into a pot of water and seasoned, you can just let it simmer. That's it. And what emerges from the depths of your stock is a glossy, dark mahogany, mysteriously herbal broth.

Equipment

1 baking sheet

1 large slow cooker, Dutch oven, or soup pot (at least 6 quarts/6 litres)

1 large strainer

1 very large bowl (4 to 5 quarts/4 to 5 litres)

1 ladle

Bone Broth

3½ pounds (1.5 kilograms) raw beef bones (or chicken or turkey bones)

2 carrots, roughly chopped

2 stalks celery, roughly chopped

1 yellow onion, roughly chopped (peels included)

2 cloves garlic, cut in half (peels included)

2 tablespoons apple cider vinegar

2 tablespoons tomato paste (for beef bones only)

2 bay leaves

1 tablespoon whole black peppercorns

2 teaspoons kosher salt

Step 1: Preheat the oven to 425°F (220°C). Place the beef bones on a baking sheet and roast for 25 to 30 minutes. This will infuse the bones with a more robust, rich flavour. If using chicken or turkey bones, skip this step.

Step 2: Place the bones in a large slow cooker, Dutch oven, or soup pot. The bones should fill three-quarters of the cooking vessel. Add the carrots, celery, onions, and garlic. Fill the remaining volume of the slow cooker or pot with water (about 12 to 16 cups/3 to 4 litres). Add the vinegar, tomato paste (if using beef bones), bay leaves, peppercorns, and salt. Cook on low for 18 hours minimum, and up to 24 hours. The longer the broth is infused with all the extra trimmings, the less broth you will have but the deeper the flavour will be. If you are cooking overnight with a Dutch oven or soup pot, you can cover the pot, place it in the refrigerator until the morning, and start where you left off when you wake.

Step 3: Once the broth is ready, set up a strainer over a very large bowl. Begin by ladling the broth over the strainer. Continue until you have had enough of the ladling and feel that lifting the pot is a safe bet. Pour the remaining broth through the strainer into the bowl and set aside to cool to room temperature, 30 to 40 minutes, before storing. A good broth will have a layer of gelatinized fat on the top once thoroughly cooled. This may not appear until the broth is chilled in the refrigerator, but as soon as you see fat layers forming, remove the fat with a spoon and discard. Taste the broth and season with salt as needed. The broth can be stored in airtight containers or sealed jars in the refrigerator for up to 1 week or in the freezer for up to 2 months.

NOTES

There are a few vegetables I would not recommend including in your stock. Pass on the cabbage, broccoli, and cauliflower. They make the broth cloudy and are much more beneficial in other recipes (see Sauerkraut on page 227 or Mushroom Garlic Pot-Stickers on page 61).

Any extra vegetable scraps you have on hand can be added into your broth.

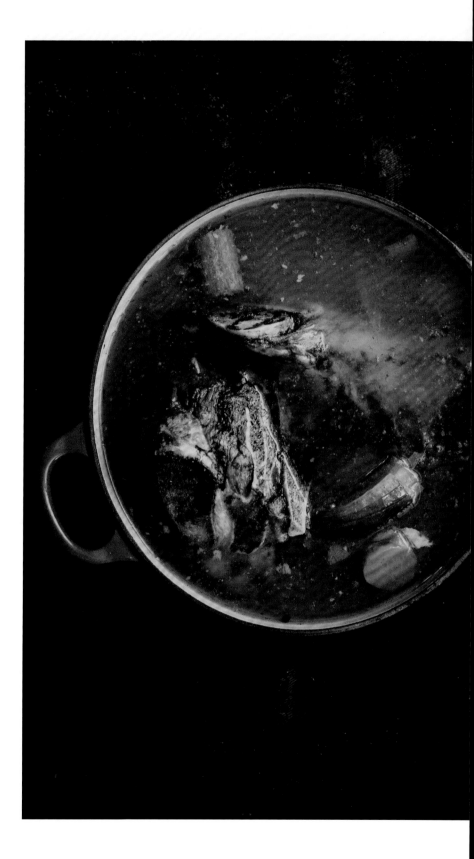

Cardamom Pear Breakfast Oats

Serves 4

A friend in university once told me that "those who eat porridge are as beige as the meal is bland." I didn't know what to make of this, as he had watched me eat my "bland" porridge every morning of that semester. I also didn't understand how one could think of porridge as bland. Sure, it is the colour beige, and yes, its name does not roll off the tongue, but bland? I do not think so! Porridge, when cooked slowly over the stove (not instant oats, but the rolled kind), develops into a delicate warm bowl full of sustenance that can feel like a well-meaning gesture on the coldest, most stressful of mornings. Yet to imply that porridge is boring is also to say that porridge is versatile! Like a blank canvas, it can take on a contrast of textures and flavours most breakfast cereals cannot, like the fruity-piney aroma of cardamom or the sweetness of a pear. Winter pears like Bosc or Anjou are best here, as they are harvested late in the season and slowly ripen until they reach their prime in January and February. The slightly crisp cardamom pears complement the soft chewiness of the porridge, and the nuts add a crunch that melds with the creaminess of yogurt. There is a lot for your mouth to experience, all of which does not include the word "bland."

1½ cups (135 grams) rolled oats

¼ teaspoon kosher salt

1½ cups (375 mL) water

1 Bosc pear (or Anjou or Bartlett), cored and cut into cubes

1 tablespoon pure maple syrup

1 teaspoon ground cardamom

¼ cup hazelnuts, crushed

2 tablespoons almonds, crushed

Oat milk (or any milk, but I like the natural sweetness of oat milk), for serving

¼ cup (60 mL) plain 2% yogurt (optional)

Preheat the oven to 350°F (175°C) and line two baking sheets with parchment paper.

In a medium pot over high heat, combine the oats, salt, and water. Once the water reaches a boil, reduce to a simmer, cover, and cook until the grains are tender and have absorbed the water, 20 to 25 minutes. Check the porridge every so often as it cooks; if the water is absorbing before the grains are tender, add ¼ cup (60 mL) water at a time and give it all a good stir.

Meanwhile, in a mixing bowl, mix together the pears, maple syrup, and cardamom. Evenly spread the pear mixture onto one of the prepared baking sheets. Roast until the pears have released a bit of juice—they will look glossy and slightly golden—20 to 22 minutes. Once out of the oven, press the pears with the back of a fork to release any remaining juices. Transfer the pears to a bowl for future porridge embellishing, and pour the juices into a separate bowl. Reserve the juice for adding to the porridge, as desired. Keep the oven on.

On the second baking sheet, evenly spread the hazelnuts and almonds. Bake for 3 to 4 minutes, until everything is toasted but not burnt (there is a small window for this, so you will need to keep a close eye on your nuts).

Once the porridge is ready, add a bit of oat milk and the excess juices from the roasted pears to thin the porridge to your desired consistency. Divide the porridge among four bowls and top with the pears, toasted hazelnuts and almonds, and a dollop of yogurt, if desired.

Old Man Sandwich on a Kaiser Roll

Serves 1

Get a sandwich right and it will satiate as successfully as any other meal. I am sure that is how my dad felt on weekend mornings while my family sat at the kitchen table and watched him perform the act of making an "old man" sandwich. It was quite the production, or so we thought at the time. He would split a kaiser roll, brush it with extra-grainy mustard, fry up a slice of bacon, fry a tomato, fork out a generous number of hot peppers—enough to make your hair stand up just looking at them—and, as if your nose isn't already tingling, add a few mustard greens. He would then proceed to lay down sharp cheese, let it melt with the addition of soft scrambled eggs, and close the sandwich with the top bun. Side note: The Old Man Sandwich is also known as the world's best breakfast for the unfortunates who may have had one glass too many the night before. Take that information as you will, and enjoy this no matter your physical state.

1 slice peameal bacon

2 large slices beefsteak tomatoes

1 tablespoon unsalted butter

2 eggs, lightly beaten

Kosher salt, to season

1 kaiser roll, cut in half

1 teaspoon grainy mustard

¼ cup mustard greens

2 to 3 thin slices sharp Cheddar

2 tablespoons pickled hot peppers

Freshly cracked black pepper, to season

Heat a small non-stick skillet over medium-high heat. Once the skillet is hot, add the bacon and cook for 3 minutes on each side. Place the bacon on a paper towel–lined plate and set aside for serving. Reduce the heat of the skillet to medium-low and fry the thick tomato slices in the bacon fat until lightly browned, 2 minutes on each side. Remove the tomato slices from the heat and set aside for serving. Wipe the skillet clean, set it over medium heat, and reheat it with the butter. Once the butter begins to soften and coat the pan, add the beaten eggs and lightly season with salt. Cook, stirring with a wooden or rubber spatula, until eggs have set into creamy folds, 1 to 2 minutes. Remove the eggs from the heat and set aside for serving.

Evenly spread the kaiser roll with the grainy mustard, adding more if desired. Add an even layer of mustard greens and top with the warm tomato slices, bacon, and thin slices of Cheddar. Top with warm scrambled eggs and garnish with the hot peppers. Season with salt and pepper to taste. Serve immediately with great pride and anticipation.

Big Lacinato Kale Salad

Serves 4

Even with frost on the ground, I will never forgo my love of leafy greens, especially long, plumed leaves of lacinato kale. Usually the last leaf standing in the winter, this is the hardiest of the kales and can withstand virtually any amount of cold. It is a leaf of many names—also known as dino kale, black kale, Tuscan kale, and Italian black cabbage—or, as my Italian friend, Allegra, says, "vero de Toscana." Its ribbed leaves do an impeccable job as the base for assertive flavours like pungent Parmesan. Lacinato's sister, green kale, is more ubiquitous at the markets, but despite being a dark leafy green too, the green variety does not hold up in the same thick, chewy way. The quantity of Parmesan in this recipe sounds alarming, but it brings the whole dish together and offers a luxurious contrast to otherwise basic ingredients. Mix it all up and sprinkle on toasted pine nuts and dried currants. This recipe technically serves four and would be great served alongside fresh pasta or pizza, but if you're like me, you may want to eat the whole bowl of salad yourself.

¼ cup pine nuts

1 bunch lacinato kale (8 cups/
  2 litres when chopped)

Kosher salt, to season

2 tablespoons white wine vinegar

¼ cup (60 mL) good-quality extra
  virgin olive oil

1 cup (3½ ounces/100 grams)
  freshly grated Parmesan, plus
  more shavings for serving

¼ cup dried currants

Heat a small skillet over medium-high. You can test the skillet by splashing a drop of water onto the surface. If the water sizzles and evaporates, it is hot enough. Add the pine nuts. Using a wooden spoon, move the pine nuts around to avoid burning them. Cook until some of the pine nuts are golden, 2 to 3 minutes. Remove from the heat and set aside.

Finely chop the kale into bite-size pieces. Do your best to shred the kale as thinly as possible. This will make it easier to soften into the oil and absorb the rich flavours of the dish. Place the kale in a large mixing bowl, at least double the size of the kale. Add the salt and vinegar and massage well with your hands. Add the oil and continue to massage the kale with your hands for 3 to 4 minutes, until wilted. Add the Parmesan and currants and give it a quick toss.

Plate the kale salad on four plates, top with the pine nuts and extra shaved Parmesan, and serve.

Crispy Homemade Fries with Harissa Ketchup

Serves a crowd

Not much would excite me more at 5 years of age than when my mom would serve me a plate stacked with thick-cut golden batons. Such a charming, nostalgic gesture that I will remember as the most delicious homemade fries I ever ate. Though my mom and I still disagree on their official title—she says "chips," whereas I say "fries"—we both agree that starchy potatoes like Yukon Gold or White Russet hold up best when frying. And with that unanimous vote, I'd recommend sticking with those potato varieties. Timing here will vary depending on the fry size and pot depth, but anyone who has eaten fries will know exactly when they are ready—a honey-brown edge and firm to the touch. Crunchy bits included.

Harissa Ketchup

3 cloves garlic, peeled

1 tablespoon kosher salt

½ cup (125 mL) plain yogurt (choose a thick Balkan or Greek yogurt)

¼ cup (60 mL) tomato paste

3 tablespoons harissa paste (see Note)

1 tablespoon ground sumac

2 tablespoons white wine vinegar

2 tablespoons honey

Crispy Homemade Fries

6 medium (2½ pounds/1 kilogram) Yukon Gold potatoes, peeled

Sunflower oil, for frying (about 10 cups/2.5 litres)

¾ teaspoon kosher salt

Flaky sea salt, to season

NOTE: *Harissa is an extremely versatile paste made of Tunisian and Libyan hot chili peppers. You can buy it at most local specialty stores, and I've seen it at a few large grocery store chains.*

In a mortar, smash the garlic and salt with a pestle. Mix in the yogurt, tomato paste, and harissa, followed by the sumac and vinegar. Mix in the honey and taste. Add a little more harissa paste and salt if you think the ketchup needs a little more piquancy. Set aside for serving. Extra harissa ketchup can be stored in a sealed container or jar and will last for up to 1 week in the refrigerator.

Using a fry cutter or knife, cut the potatoes into evenly sized ½-inch (1 cm) fries.

Pour the sunflower oil into a deep, heavy pot until the oil is at least 3 inches (8 cm) deep. Heat over medium. Use a cooking thermometer to check the heat; once the temperature reaches 250°F (120°C), add half of the potatoes. Cook until the fries are crispy and golden on the outside, 15 to 20 minutes. Remove with a spider strainer or slotted spoon. (If the fries fall apart when you remove them, they need another 3 to 5 minutes of cooking.) Spread the fries single file on a baking sheet and set aside. Check the temperature of the oil once more to ensure the temperature has not dropped below 250°F (120°C), and adjust heat if it has. Add the remainder of the potatoes to the pot of oil. Repeat the process.

Transfer the fries with a spider strainer or slotted spoon to a large stainless-steel bowl. Add the kosher salt and toss well. (Everybody has a different take on how much salt makes a good plate of fries, so you will need to taste and finish with a seasoning of flaky sea salt as desired.) Serve with the harissa ketchup.

Peak Season Ramen

Serves 4

Toronto has a dynamic Japanese community, and the commitment to noteworthy ramen restaurants shows no bounds. Deeming one "the best" is simply impossible. Though, if you are looking for a really spectacular experience, the ramen at Nobuya in Etobicoke is complex and unique. I recommend serving this ramen hot and topping with an array of veggies: mixed mushrooms, bok choy, and green onions.

2 tablespoons canola oil

3 cups mixed mushrooms (like portobello, shiitake, cremini, and enoki), sliced into ¼-inch (0.5 cm) pieces

1 clove garlic, minced

1 teaspoon minced fresh ginger

2 teaspoons tamari

2 teaspoons red wine vinegar

1 handful fresh cilantro, roughly chopped, divided

2 eggs

6 cups (1.5 litres) Bone Broth (page 248)

1 pound (450 grams) ramen noodles (fresh or dry; see Note)

2 baby bok choy, quartered

¼ cup chopped green onions (cut into ½-inch/1 cm strips)

1 teaspoon dried chili flakes (optional)

NOTE: *You can find fresh ramen noodles at Asian supermarkets and some Chinese restaurants. Fresh noodles are best to absorb all the flavours, but dry can be found in most grocery stores.*

Heat a large skillet over medium-high. Add the oil and mushrooms. Allow the mushrooms to brown on one side before flipping, about 4 minutes. Flip and continue cooking for another 3 to 4 minutes. Reduce the heat to medium and add the garlic and ginger, stirring often. Sauté until fragrant, about 3 minutes. Pour in the tamari and vinegar and mix. Toss in half of the cilantro and stir until wilted. Remove the skillet from the heat and set aside.

To boil the eggs, heat a medium pot filled with water over high. Once the water reaches a rolling boil, turn the heat off, gently submerge the eggs, and place the lid on the pot. For a jammy yolk, leave the eggs in the hot water for 4 to 6 minutes before removing them and rinsing under cold water to stop them from cooking any longer. Once the eggs are cool enough to handle, peel and set aside for serving.

For Fresh Ramen Noodles: Heat the broth in a medium pot over high, until the broth reaches a boil. Ladle the broth into four bowls. In a separate pot, bring water to a rolling boil. Add the fresh ramen noodles and reduce the heat to medium. Cook the noodles for 1½ minutes. Strain the noodles and divide them into the four bowls of broth. Top each with a generous amount of mushrooms, the remaining cilantro, bok choy, green onions, and half a boiled egg. Sprinkle with chili flakes before serving.

For Dry Ramen Noodles: Heat the broth in a medium pot over high, until the broth reaches a boil. While you are waiting for the broth to heat, divide the ramen noodles evenly between four bowls. Ladle the hot broth over the noodles and top each with a generous amount of mushrooms, the remaining cilantro, bok choy, green onions, and half a boiled egg. Sprinkle with chili flakes before serving.

The Classic Poutine with Bone Broth Gravy

Serves 4

I couldn't write a cookbook about what we eat in Ontario without including a poutine recipe. This is what got me through the coldest of winters on the ski hill. What gets you down a hill in −30°C (−22°F) is the prospect of warming up in a fogged window chalet, ready to hold a plate of crispy potatoes covered in nuggets of cheese half melted from the hot gravy blanketing the entire dish. Every fry you pick, you hope to pull a long string of cheese—the length of your arm to your mouth. And when served with hot chocolate, this is the most comforting meal for a Canadian skier. A very classic poutine with a slightly (I said slightly) healthier gravy made from your own homemade bone broth.

Bone Broth Gravy

3 tablespoons potato starch (or organic corn starch)

2⅓ cups (580 mL) Bone Broth (page 248), divided

3 cloves garlic, minced

1 large yellow onion, roughly chopped

Kosher salt and freshly cracked black pepper

Poutine

1 batch Crispy Homemade Fries (page 256)

1½ pounds (675 grams) cheese curds

In a small bowl, whisk the potato starch with ⅓ cup (80 mL) bone broth until well combined. Set aside.

Meanwhile, in a medium-size saucepan over high, heat the garlic, onions, and remaining 2 cups (500 mL) bone broth. Continually stir with a whisk until the broth comes to a boil. Reduce heat to low. Stir in the potato starch mixture and let simmer, continuing to stir, for 10 minutes or until the gravy thickens. Season with salt and pepper. Transfer the gravy to a blender and blend on low speed until smooth. Pour the blended gravy back into the saucepan to reheat when ready for serving.

To serve, plate the fries on four wide plates or shallow bowls. Crumble the cheese curds evenly across all four plates and pour the gravy on top while it is still hot; this will allow the cheese to become melty and stringy. Serve and enjoy.

Honey Pecorino Chicories

Makes 20 pieces

There is nothing more satisfying than mustering up a simple dish of seasonal ingredients—in February. It may sound like a difficult task but have you ever heard of chicories? Chicories reach their peak in cooler climates and have more ardour than most other lettuces. Varieties like Belgian endive and Treviso radicchio are bitter, long leaves that curl at the edges, much like a silky boat—all too perfect for holding a pungent cheese like Pecorino. That may seem like a lot of strong personalities, but the two complement each other well. Once we add a little sweetness of honey into the mix, all balance is restored.

1 head Belgian endive, stem and outer leaves removed

1 head Treviso radicchio, stem and outer leaves removed

3½ ounces (100 grams) Pecorino

2 teaspoons honey

2 tablespoons good-quality extra virgin olive oil

Flaky sea salt or finishing salt, to season

Pick the leaves off the heads of endive and radicchio, one by one, until you have about 20 boat-shaped leaves. Cut the Pecorino into 20 slices so thin you can read through them—about ¼ inch (0.5 cm) thick (I like to use a mandoline or peeler for this). Arrange the leaves on a platter. Place one slice of Pecorino inside each leaf. Drizzle with a bit of honey and olive oil. Sprinkle each boat with salt and serve.

Pancetta Parsnip Gnocchi with Toasted Pecans & Radicchio

Serves 4

Though gnocchi can be seen as a simple entry into good pasta making, there are some details that can't be missed: a good-quality dough and a gentle but confident hand, and you must cook more than is needed for one meal. A parsnip may seem an odd choice to incorporate into gnocchi, but I stand firm on this, especially in February when the gentle sweetness of these barks-of-a-birch-tree-looking roots come into their own. This is a rich root vegetable that marries well with potatoes and adds a layer of nutty sweetness to already silky-smooth gnocchi. And just for a little contrast, the bitter leaves of a cold-weather chicory, like a crimson-red radicchio, go well here. Leftovers are excellent seared and served with butter, a little garlic, a few toasted pecans, and more bitter greens if you like.

Parsnip Potato Gnocchi

3 cloves garlic, roughly chopped

½ pound (225 grams) parsnips, peeled and roughly quartered

1½ pounds (680 grams) Idaho or Russet potatoes, peeled and quartered

2 eggs, beaten

1 cup (130 grams) "00" flour, plus more for dusting

¼ cup (0.9 ounce/25 grams) freshly grated Pecorino or Parmesan

1 head radicchio, stem and outer leaves removed

4 slices pancetta, cut into ¼-inch (0.5 cm) pieces

¼ cup pecans

Good-quality extra virgin olive oil, for serving

Zest and juice of 1 lemon, for garnish

Freshly grated Parmesan, for serving

Flaky sea salt, for serving

Make the Parsnip Potato Gnocchi: Preheat the oven to 350°F (175°C) and line a baking sheet with parchment paper.

Bring a large pot of lightly salted water to a boil. Add the garlic, parsnips, and potatoes. Boil until the parsnips and potatoes are tender, 25 to 30 minutes. Remove the parsnips and potatoes from the pot of boiling water and set the pot aside, along with the water, for later use.

Spread the parsnips and potatoes on the prepared baking sheet and bake for 10 minutes to dry them out. Place them in a large bowl and mash them while they are still warm until fluffy. Form a well in the centre of the mashed vegetables, ensuring the mash has now cooled enough to touch. Pour in the beaten eggs, flour, and cheese and begin to mix with your hands. Knead gently until a soft dough forms. Set aside for 10 minutes to rest.

On a clean, dusted work surface, divide and roll the dough into eight snake-like ropes, about the thickness of your thumb. Cut the ropes into many ¾-inch (2 cm) pieces. Lightly dust the gnocchi pillows with flour.

To shape the gnocchi, hold a fork at a 90-degree angle from tine to counter. With the other hand, lightly but assertively use your thumb to press and roll the gnocchi pillow down the fork end. The gnocchi will curl into the shape of a *C*. Set the gnocchi pillow aside and repeat.

recipe continues

To cook the gnocchi, bring the large pot of salted water used previously back to a boil. Drop a batch of 20 gnocchi pillows into the water and cook. Once they are cooked, they will rise to the surface of the water. After 10 seconds of surfacing, use a slotted spoon to scoop the gnocchi out of the water and lay them across the baking sheet. Continue this process until all the gnocchi are cooked.

Finish the Dish: Pick the leaves off the head of radicchio, one by one, until you have 15 to 20 leaves. (If the leaves are bigger than your thumbs, tear each leaf into bite-size pieces.) Equally distribute leaves onto four plates.

Line a plate with paper towel and set beside the stove. Heat a skillet over medium heat and cook the pancetta until crispy, 3 to 5 minutes. Remove the pancetta from the skillet and place on the lined plate. Reduce the heat to low and toast the pecans in the pancetta fat until lightly browned, 2 to 3 minutes. Remove the pecans from the heat and set aside on the lined plate with the pancetta.

While the skillet is still hot and the pancetta fat remains warm, add the boiled gnocchi to the skillet and reheat over medium to give the gnocchi a golden bottom, about 5 minutes. Gently remove the gnocchi from the skillet and spoon over the plates of radicchio. This will give the radicchio a gentle wilt. Drizzle each plate with good-quality olive oil, then garnish with a splash of lemon juice, a sprinkle of lemon zest, a handful of freshly grated Parmesan, pancetta crisps, and toasted pecans. Taste to season with flaky sea salt and serve.

Meet the Team: A Glossary, of Sorts

SOME SEASONAL AND SPECIALTY INGREDIENTS in this book may be known to you, while others might be new. Here's a listing of the less common items and where to find them.

Beluga lentils: You can find these lentils at most organic grocery stores, at some superstores, at some local specialty stores, and online.

Black garlic: These bulbs can be found at Korean specialty stores, Chinese supermarkets, and most farmers' markets year-round.

Blossoming chives: Chives with purple flowers still on their heads are available at farmers' markets in June and July. Regular chives work just as well.

Calabrese peppers: These Italian peppers also go by the name peperoncini or peperoncino. You can find this pepper in its fresh, whole form in Italian specialty stores or jarred in oil at most superstores.

Dried unsulphered fruits: Most bulk stores will carry these. So will organic specialty stores.

Edible lavender: Most bulk stores and organic specialty stores will carry this form of lavender. If you live in Ontario, I recommend visiting a lavender farm in June to see the purple fields and buy edible lavender there. It's a nice day trip.

Fiddleheads: Native to Ontario and available for about 6 weeks of the year. You can find these emerald-green spirals from mid-April through the end of May at farmers' markets, some CSA (community-supported agriculture) programs, most superstores, and local specialty stores.

Garlic scapes: The spirally greens plucked from the garlic bulb show up in June at farmers' markets and stores that specialize in local produce. I have also started to see them at superstores. They are growing in popularity, and I predict they will be more prevalent in the coming years.

Gochujang: This sweet, spicy, and savoury chili paste is used often in Korean cooking and can be found in Korean grocery stores and some superstores.

Ground cherries: These marble-sized orange fruits are tart and sweet, with a husk similar to a tomatillo. Come summer, they can be purchased at almost every superstore, farmers' market, and local specialty store (see Note, page 76).

Harissa paste: This smoky, spicy, and tangy chili-garlic paste is used most commonly in Tunisian cooking. You can find it at local specialty stores, North African specialty stores, and organic specialty stores. I have recently seen it in major superstores.

Hickory chips: Used for smoking, you can find these in most superstores (you may need to ask) and hardware stores.

Horseradish (fresh): Most superstores and Eastern European specialty stores carry the fresh variety.

Kimchi: Cabbage and radish are most famously used to make kimchi, a popular fermented and salted vegetable dish in Korea. It can be found in Korean grocery stores, local specialty stores, and most superstores.

Maitake mushrooms: Also known as hen-of-the-woods, these mushrooms can be found at some farmers' markets, superstores, and local specialty stores.

Masa flour: This finely ground flour is made of dried corn and used most often for tortillas, tamales, and pupusas. It can be found at almost every superstore, at some local specialty stores, at Mexican specialty stores, and online.

Mulberries: Mulberries can be found on the tree-lined streets of Toronto. Some farmers' markets with a forager vendor will have them in June, but in case you can't find them, I have provided some alternatives in the recipes.

Nettles: Most people consider this spring green a weed. Nettles sting, so many people stay away, but they are rich and earthy and taste similar to spinach. You can find them at farmers' markets and grocery stores that specialize in local produce from May to September.

Oyster mushrooms: Superstores, farmers' markets, grocery stores that specialize in local food, and some CSAs will have oyster mushrooms throughout the year.

Ramen noodles (fresh): These can be found at Asian specialty stores and supermarkets, as well as some Chinese restaurants.

Red fife flour: Canada's oldest wheat variety and heritage grain is nutty and earthy and gives baked goods a savoury depth of flavour. You can find it at most specialty local stores, some CSAs, and some local bakers.

Pasta (fresh): This can be found at Italian specialty stores.

Romanesco broccoli: This green geometric broccoli castle can be found at farmers' markets, local specialty stores, and some superstores from November to January.

Rose water: Almost every superstore carries this.

Shichimi togarashi: The Japanese name of this zesty, toasty, and salty spice mix translates to "7 flavours" in English. Many superstores, some local specialty stores, and Japanese specialty stores carry this spice. And when all else fails, you can make your own (see Note, page 132).

Sumac: This red flower dried and ground into a tart, citrusy seasoning is available in most superstores, bulk stores, and spice stores.

Sunchokes: Also known as Jerusalem artichokes, sunchokes are native to Ontario. They are harvested in the fall and can be found throughout the winter at farmers' markets, local specialty stores, CSAs, and, more recently, superstores.

Tomatillos: These look like green tomatoes with husks. They are not quite a tomato but are cousins in the Solanaceae family. They appear at farmers' markets and local specialty stores in the summer. Some superstores will also carry tomatillos between July and September.

Walnut oil: This is a good finishing oil that imparts its nutty, sweet flavours into a meal. Most grocery stores will have it, and organic/specialty stores will definitely have it.

Wild leeks: Also known as ramps in Ontario, these appear in April at farmers' markets, some superstores, and grocery stores that specialize in local produce.

NOTE ON ORGANIC: Buying organic is not always an option for everyone, but if organic choices are available and you can afford them, make them a priority. The soil, your body, and your taste buds will be much happier for it.

Acknowledgements

ALL OF THE "THANK YOUS" THAT I EXPRESS HERE will need to be multiplied a million times over because I am profoundly grateful to everyone who has encouraged me throughout this journey.

Thank you immensely to my editor, Rachel Brown, for your endless amount of guidance, precision, and patience. From the beginning, you got it. You understood that I have written this book from my heart, and as an author, I have always felt I was in the best hands. You made a home for my work and for that I am incredibly thankful. A big thank-you to the entire Appetite team for your love and support.

To Janette, the photographer of these beautiful images and beloved friend. Thank you for filling every shoot day with your bottomless kindness and warm spirit. You saw my vision and helped me bring every recipe on these pages to life. Between all of the laughter and dancing, I am not quite sure how we got anything done but maybe that is part of the magic of creating with you.

To Candice, the world's best illustrator and loyal confidant. Thank you for the most endearing images sprinkled throughout this book, and more importantly, the gift of our friendship. Life knowing you has been rich and blessed. You have been a never-ending champion for my work. You buoyed me up from the beginning, when the book was just a seed and a wall of sticky notes scattered across kitchen cupboards. You have always had an unwavering confidence in me and for that I am forever grateful.

Thank you to my family and friends who were there through the good, the bad, and the sometimes too-dry tarts. You have been a good balance of honest critics who humble and encourage me to refine my recipes, as well as rave reviewers who stroked my bruised ego. I know this book is good because it now has your stamp of approval on it. A special thanks to Liz, Mark, and Oscar for always having an open door when I shuttled in the hundredth plate of test-kitchen meals for you to take off of my hands. You welcomed every dish with open arms.

Thank you, Caitlin, for making the stunning ceramics for this book. You are a spark of endless generosity. Thank you for lending us your studio for our shoots, for all of the ceramics that you provided, and for your never stifling creativity. I remember many moons back, when I was just starting out and found myself drawn into Cylinder Studio, you said to me that I was going to make delicious things and capture it one day. Thank you for knowing this before I did.

To Rick, my literary agent, for guiding and representing me through the not-so-intuitive process of my first book.

To everyone at Fresh City Farms. You are a major foundation of this book. A special thanks to: Ran, for your continued faith in my work and support of my career; Abra, for being the greatest model of patience and steadiness. You make every day a joy to work with you and to know you; Jenn, for always challenging me (in the most encouraging ways) in the kitchen. I do not care how many months and trials it took us to develop that strawberry smoothie, we got it just right! Words cannot describe how lucky I am to have you all in my corner.

Thank you to my Fjällräven family for your endless community support.

To my kitchen helpers, Olivia, Jeff, Irene, and Mom. I am forever grateful for the amount of onions we had to chop together and dishes we had to put away. The best conversations are always over the kitchen sink. And thank you for eating all of the food we cooked. There was no way I could do that on my own.

To all of the farmers I know. It takes real courage and fortitude to be a steward of the land, to labour over your fields, to champion for a healthier world, and to go unacknowledged, by many, for it. You are all celebrities to me. You have not only sold me ingredients but you have encased a story of hard work, dedication, and some damn good ingredients. Every time I see you, you provide a wisdom, a generosity, and pure edible education that inspires me to rush home and cook with what you have grown.

It would be impossible to list all of the farmers who make me eager to buy their food on a daily basis, but I can try: Alexandra and Jorge from OsoLeo Wildcrafters, Alison Chris from Lady Cone Hop Yards, Jim from Haystrom Farm, Audrey from Greenhouse Eatery, Irina and Jon from Bees Universe, Daniel from The Cutting Veg, Julianne at Fresh City Farms, Jessica from Lunar Rhythm Gardens, Milan and Nacho from Bizjak Farms, Dave and Emily Kendal Hills Farm, Annette from Organic Vibes, Tony from Wheelbarrow Farm, Liz and Matt from Joyfully Organic Farm, and all of the other farmers who have provided such nourishments to this book. To all of you, thank you. You are a part of an infinitely larger spirit. Thank you to the markets and grocers that sell local food, and every shopper buying it.

Lastly, thank you to all bookshops, those who work in them, and everyone who enters their local bookstores. To hold and smell a book in hand is a beautiful thing.

Thank you, readers, for your support and cooking in peak season.

Index